America's Customer Service Disaster
- A Perfect Storm

To My Amazing Family

Sandra
Christina
Moke
Jay
Baby

'A perfect storm is an event in which a rare combination of circumstances drastically aggravates the event.

The term is used by analogy to an unusually severe storm that results from a rare combination of meteorological phenomena'

Forward

by Homer Rice
Former Head Coach, Cincinnati Bengals
Director of Athletics, University of North Carolina, University of Cincinnati, Rice University, Georgia Tech
Adjunct Professor – Leadership Fitness – Georgia Tech

Paul Karem, the author of ABOVE THE FRAY, produced many successes in various businesses that have molded him into a Positive Leader. His service excellence mandate in the mortgage industry made him a leading, record setting originator and an inspiration, enabling many associates to achieve their own success. His unique style of leadership and understanding of the customer made him an inspiration in the industry. A man of high principles, Paul is respected as the one at the top of the ladder.

As with all top leaders, Paul pledged his time to others. One example is his role as the Executive Producer of BLACK IN BLUE, a documentary film about the breaking of race barriers in the Southeastern Conference, a story which includes Paul's African American teammates at the University of Kentucky. Paul created this film project, garnered the financing and recruited Paul Wagner, an Academy Award winning filmmaker for creation of the film. It was through this "giving" that I reconnected with Paul. I served as the Offensive Coordinator of the University of Kentucky football program from 1962-1965. Kentucky did not have a single African American athlete in any sport at that time and neither did any other Southeastern Conference Institution. I was involved in recruiting a young football player from Middlesboro, Kentucky, Greg Page in 1964 and 1965. Greg became the first African American to sign a Southeastern Conference letter of intent---for ANY sport. Others followed Greg at Kentucky to break the barrier and set the tone for the other conference schools. Paul, a former quarterback for the Wildcats, created the mission to make sure that this story is told and that these courageous young men are recognized as pioneers that took the first step.

Someone once said, "Success is not measured by your climbing the ladder of success but by the number of people you helped climb that ladder." If this is true—and I believe it is—then Paul Karem is certainly one of the most successful leaders I have been privileged to know.

I encourage you to read this book and join many others whom Paul Karem has enlightened with a new awareness about customer service excellence. You will be astonished with how you can use these lessons, what you can do with them, and ultimately what you can achieve.

Table of Contents

Edited by Jody Gilbert

America's Customer Service Disaster - A Perfect Storm

Chapter One: Introduction

America has nicknames for many periods in her history. We have the Roaring Twenties, when everybody enjoyed peace, flappers, and illegal whiskey. The Golden Age of Sports blessed us with Babe Ruth, Jack Dempsey, and a Triple Crown winner in Gallant Fox, all in the same era. Manufacturing suppliers in the Civil War performed so poorly (soles falling off boots and coats and jackets falling apart) that the moniker for that age was The Age of Shoddy. The likelihood is that, in years to come when the current, dreadful era of customer service has passed, it will be labeled The Age of Rude. Or maybe The Age of Indifference, or The Age of Phone Trees.

Never before in the history of American free enterprise have the stars been in such perfect alignment as they are at this time for the current customer service *disaster*.

A perfect storm has created this event, this era. Wikipedia defines a perfect storm as an event in which a rare combination of circumstances drastically aggravates the event. Well, if that's what it takes to make a perfect storm, then we are in one right now.

Just as there has been an unholy increase in the depletion of individual customer service skills, discourteous behavior, and indifference to troubled customer situations, we are at the advent of an emerging technology replacing the same people who lack those skills. The problem with that is, the technology doesn't have the customer service skills either—or at least the people implementing the technology don't know how to use it to simulate those skills. Seniors are having trouble with phone trees, keeping track of multiple ID and PIN numbers, and are driven mad by the absence of helpful compunction when *finally* reaching a human voice.

Millennials, once the scourge of those pining for more customer service help, are now just as marinated in frustration as Seniors—even though they are levels and levels ahead in attempting to penetrate the nearly impenetrable wall of technology that separates the customer from resolution. Millennials, as well as the generations before and after them, are pounding the table for better, more reactive, technology. I believe I am qualified to make that statement on Millennials for this reason: When I first launched my dialogue and efforts toward a discussion about customer service, my daughters, upon viewing or reading my musings, regularly responded with "Dad, no one cares about that crap!" Now, as successful businesswomen, both JoAnna and Christina find the same frustration we all do with exasperating, bad customer service. Chat rooms temporarily solved the problem for Millennials but soon they were out of vogue in favor of "Live" chat rooms. All part of the search for courteous, empathetic, earnest help.

A gentleman named Gordon Matthews started working on an idea in the late seventies that he believed would benefit and fortify businesses. He decided to call his idea "voice mail." Matthews, who had 35 patents at the time of his death, received a patent for the voice mail invention in 1982. He formed a company called VMX, which stands for Voice Message Express, and eventually sold that company to 3M, which in turn sold it to a company named Octel Communications.

When the product was launched, only the largest and most successful companies engaged in voice mail because of the burdensome expense. Some years later, with the advance of PC-based processing boards, voice mail was everywhere, dropped on American business like an anvil out of the sky. And company after company, large and small, successful and floundering, in all industries, welcomed the anvil into their offices.

One big problem with accepting the anvil: No one knew, and for my money most still don't know, how to use it. The idea Mr. Gordon had was voice *mail*—mail being something you read and respond to. With voice mail, the response is often limited to "returning your call" or "call me back, tag you're it" instead of responding in a precise manner to the original call by composing your response in verbal MAIL. A proper response addresses all the issues voiced on the received phone call and responds to them in a specific nature. It doesn't leave messages back and forth for two days, which is *exactly* what happens. Over and over and over. No one responds to a written letter by writing back and saying "Got your letter, will write you back."

To this day, phone recordings and phone trees remain the most frustrating, maddening issue for customer satisfaction. Brad Tuttle, in the July 29, 2015, edition of *Money* magazine, reported that 75% of customer service complaints are due to people being "highly annoyed" when they can't get a live person on the phone to help with a problem. The point is this: Regardless of the ingenuity behind voice mail, people want to talk to a live person, especially in a critical situation. And regardless of the ingenuity of the product, very few still use it effectively. It ain't working. You can see by a quick look at Mr. Tuttle's article that the numbers, and the problem, are worsening.

I recall accepting a terrific offer in 1994 to run the mortgage division of a bank. A great company with great, talented people. Having come from a bank/mortgage division that had remarkable customer service and remarkable teamwork, I was startled by an initial observation at my new job—something that hit me in the forehead like a shovel: Why don't people here answer the phone? Well, the reason was, they were using this new thing called voice mail. And with the use of voice mail, somehow answering the phone while it was ringing had gone out the window. As we'll discuss later in this book, voice mail allowed the receiver of the call to set her or his own pace about reacting to the call. Voice mail, the wonderful invention of Gordon Matthews, did not succeed in its mission of speeding up and adding efficiency to communication—it stopped it.

Anatomy of the Customer Service Disaster

While the voice mail component, only a small part of the technology piece of America's Customer Service Disaster, is raging and building, it is joined by another tsunami of America's Customer Service Disaster. Thin-skinned behavior. We are in a time of massive division politically, socially, and financially—possibly more than ever before. Those differences, often based in judgmental politics, have hit the ground in business etiquette—hard.

Soft skills are not taught effectively in most schools and not only that, in some quarters are looked upon as politically insensitive. What should be considered the most critical requirement of business success has morphed into "kissing someone's behind" or "humbling" oneself. The real truth is that regardless of the training, certifications, or degrees one might have, if a person doesn't know how to deliver those products in an effective dialogue with customers, those accomplishments are not worth the paper they are written on.

A second contributor to America's Customer Service Disaster is the misuse of technology. Consider the *Business Insider* article by Doug Clinton from February 7, 2018. The title of the article is "Automation will make customer service the most in-demand job in tech"—man that is bad news for techies who think they're not going to have to deal directly with disgruntled customers. With the certain emergence of successful customer intimacy connections in technology, it still will fall to a human to close the deal. "Please listen closely, as our menu options have changed," and "This call may be recorded for quality assurance purposes," and similar ineffective uses of technology have fallen out of the sky and landed in just about every large business just like voice mail did. You can rest assured that they are soon to go to the wayside, not only for their total ineffectiveness and total waste of time but also as a result of consumer demands for better direction and more immediate help.

Just as thin-skinned behavior and the misuse of technology have hit the American business landscape in lockstep, they brought another buddy along—the Disconnect. The Disconnect is the gap between the claims service providers make about their goods and services and the gap between those claims and the way their goods and services are really delivered. Usually the worst offenders ordain that Disconnect handsomely with near-invective thin-skinned behavior and horribly misused technology. A golden hat trick. Typically, the most self-laudatory have the largest gap— the largest Disconnect. As you are reading this you are probably rattling some of those off in your mind as a result of your experiences. For me the very worst, due to personal experience, are Delta Airlines and Spectrum.

I have never had a Delta flight where everything went according to Hoyle. Not a single time. Therefore, listening to the haughty whispers of Donald Sutherland trying to convince the listener of the Delta commitment to its flyers does not get off the ground with me. The ad is called "Tell the World" and is part of the airline's "Keep Climbing" campaign, as first reported by *Adweek.*

The 60-second spot comes across less uplifting and more ominous than anything else. Donald Sutherland instills it with a powerful but somber tone. "Once you get out here, that's all there is. There's just one direction: Forward. One time: Now," he says. "And there's just one sound: You and us, together, with a mighty roar, that tells the world we're coming for you."

Haughty. Ominous. Just like waiting on the tarmac.

And Spectrum tells you with their media ads that they just about invented cable. It is easy to google the Spectrum universe of customer reviews and complaints to see the Disconnect they've authored. Or, if you dare, call them.

Lexington, KY, at one time had a city-wide contract with Spectrum cable. One of the pitches Spectrum blurts out on their TV ads goes like this: "We are REDEFINING what cable can be." The level of customer service was so bad in Lexington that it became necessary to arrange a public hearing so locals could vent their frustration with the city's cable and internet service provider. At that meeting the mayor of Lexington, Jim Gray, declared, "Every time I see the Spectrum commercial on TV I want to run my head into the television." But let's not pick on Delta and Spectrum. After all, they are just a small part of a giant gaggle, *redefining* America's Customer Service Disaster.

There you have it. A perfect storm called America's Customer Service Disaster. We are being assaulted by a three-pronged front: thin-skinned behavior, a misuse of technology, and a disconnect in ad claims from service and goods providers.

Now for the good, the great news. America's Customer Service Disaster brings an opportunity for businesses and individuals to reach, and surpass, goals and dreams like never before. In the following chapters we will review each piece of America's Customer Service Disaster and provide some answers.

Chapter Two: Thin-skinned behavior

How did we become so defensive in our current societal setting? How is it that our social, political, and financial divides have trickled into business and become rallying points for divisiveness rather than unification? No one can tell the story better than Jasky Singh.

Consider his article in *The Mission*, titled "Welcome to the Thin-Skinned Generation, Where Everything Is a Bloody Problem." In this remarkable and revealing piece, Singh explains, "These examples show why a path towards becoming hypersensitive is being laid out with clear signage and beautiful landscaping, whereas the one leading towards the essential trait of life success—'GRIT' is surrounded by shrubbery, mist, and is virtually indecipherable."

The examples he is talking about are the "drilling" of oversensitivity into the hearts and minds of children—that we are teaching children that even the slightest thing should be taken as inappropriate or offensive. He goes on to say, "I am finding it harder and harder to spot people and policies that teach grit, resilience, determination, and strength. Developing tough, snake-like, impenetrable skin. Like ****** warriors."

Here are stories that illustrate the presence of thin-skinned behavior in our current business setting, and some solutions; all of the following stories were either posted by me on my website, www.paulkarem.com, or sent in by bruised-up, frustrated consumers.

The Disney secret

The other day, someone asked me the following question:

"How is it that Disney employees are always able to provide such amazing customer service? At the rides, hotels, and the restaurants? It's uncanny!"

Well, I know the answer.

They have a secret tool. A secret device. It's not really a secret; it just seems that way because nobody uses the tool anymore.

Let me explain.

Many moons ago, our daughters reached the perfect age to go to Disney World. At the time, I was a terrified airplane passenger. I was a white-knuckle flyer and it would take me five (5) martinis to endure a one hour flight.

So I visited our family doctor and said, "I don't want my children to see what I do to myself on an airplane. Please give me something so I can tolerate the flight." The good doctor gave me a mild sedative and told me "not to take more than two of these and do not drink."

I didn't obey his orders.

I washed down multiple pills with multiple vodkas on the rocks. That's how terrified I was of flying at the time. Side note: This has since been cured by the US Air fearful flyers seminar.

We arrive in Orlando and I am an unholy mess. Arriving at Disney World is confusing in and of itself. Just an FYI: Throwing in three sedatives and three vodka rocks doesn't make it any less difficult.

We make our way to the Contemporary Hotel (Disney) and get checked in. Everyone is having a blast, but it was a long night for yours truly. I woke up at 6:30 the next morning to a horrendous headache. Meanwhile, the tribe is still sleeping. I go down to get some coffee and attempt to get myself together. I find myself in the lobby, where there are approximately 15 check-in bays (think a bank teller's station).

Every 15-20 minutes, a plane bound for Disney World lands. And every 15-20 minutes, a new batch of confused and sometimes mad travelers enters the lobby of the Contemporary Hotel to check in. They're frustrated because they don't know where to go. They have passes and reservations for special deals but have no idea which direction to go to take advantage of them. It's like a scene from *The Walking Dead*, where zombies walk around clueless without any sense of direction.

As I'm slowly coming back to life, I witness the tool.

As each hotel guest arrives fussing and huffing, the front desk agents allow them to get their ya ya's out and they just listen. They just let them vent. Then, with a smile on their face and a smile in their voice, they explain everything to the guests in a courteous, unhurried manner. And the guests go away smiling and waving at the hotel agent, exchanging pleasantries like "Thank you so much, Jennifer," and "Hope to see you later," and "I'll say hello to Pluto for you!"

Many of us start out each day with a similar thought. Something like, "I hope today is a good day and I don't have to deal with any difficult people." That's not what's going through the minds of the check-in clerks at the Contemporary Hotel. They aren't worried if the customers are belligerent or not, because they have the "tool." They know their customers are going to be unhappy.

And here is the secret: They KNOW they are going to take care of it. They know they have the skill and patience to fix it. They know the guests are going to walk away happy. So they don't have to worry about running into problematic customers. They've got the tool.

It's called customer service. It's the confidence of knowing you have the gift to please the agitated customer. It's not being insulted by someone who jumps in your grill because they are discombobulated. It is enjoying the pleasure of fixing their confusion and their problem instead of being thin-skinned and defensive. And believe me when I tell you the tool is not widely used. With that comes a way for you to succeed in your dream job or your dream career or your dream.

USE "THE TOOL" WHEN-EVER YOU LIKE. IT'S FREE!

And here is another one:

The ringleader, the follower, and the protégé

My wife and I have the good fortune to be able to do our business at a few different banks. In some ways they are all the same, and in some ways, they are 180 degrees different. They all seem to offer the same products. Free checking, itty-bitty rates on certificates of deposit, nice internet banking options, cookies in the lobby, and all the other standard banking items.

Where they differ GREATLY is in the people category. One of the banks we deal with regularly, at least for now, has an unsolvable conundrum. This particular bank has a bad combination of tellers regarding customer service. Of all the times my wife or I have walked into this bank, we have never been greeted by name and rarely, if ever, greeted at all—and neither are any of their other customers warmly greeted. It just has a bad internal synergy and it probably cannot be fixed.

And here's why it can't be fixed:

The Ringleader is in full command.

The senior teller at the bay on the end is the Ringleader. She has clearly laid down all the laws of behavior in the bank. Her countenance resonates throughout the teller line and you can bet the other tellers perform accordingly. The Ringleader has an heir in place for her position and that is the Follower. The Follower is fixated at the bay next to the Ringleader, and she follows the behavior of the Ringleader chapter and verse. Woe to the Follower should she stray from the behavioral manual and greet or smile at a customer. Should that happen, the Follower would be subjected to social damnation within the bank social structure.

The Ringleader is very good at her teachings. I have seen her in action when the Branch Manager is in the area and in that instance, she goes from Mrs. Hyde to the sweet Dr. Jekyll.

In the presence of the Branch Manager, the Ringleader smiles, greets, and asks her stunned co-workers if she can help them with anything. This graduate level technique is slowly morphing into the DNA of the other tellers.

The third teller in the conundrum is the Protégé. The Protégé is actually a victim of the Ringleader and the Follower. The Protégé has the natural urge to be kind and warm and courteous, but she is under surveillance when the Ringleader is present. The Protégé has been shrunk down by the surroundings and it's unlikely that she can break away and go with her helpful instincts.

We are going to switch to a different bank pretty soon. Too bad the Protégé can't switch, too—she would probably do very well with a positive Ringleader.

Here's the bad part about this conundrum:

- You recruit what you already have.
- The Ringleader has the high ground, and she ain't giving it up.

Solutions

Know who you are dealing with. There are many self-assessment tests available to you that can tell you a lot about yourself—and they are often remarkably accurate.

If you take a personality test, you may discover that you are one of four personality types. There are no right or wrong answers and there are no "good" or "bad" personality types. All have great, good, and not-so-good people, so don't worry about one label or the other. The personality types are amiable, driver, analytical, and expressive. Take a test. A number of good things will come from it:

- You will better embrace your assets.

- You will know how to deal with the other types.

- You will be able to identify types and react to them appropriately and effectively.

All of these techniques are good tools for eliminating thin-skinned behavior. For example: analyticals are interested only in facts and figures. Amiables, on the other hand, are nicer and easier to approach. Don't use the same smiley, back-patting on an analytical that you might on an amiable. It won't go well. Learning the keys to addressing different personality types is a great path to helping the difficult or disgruntled customer—especially if you don't have the instinctive talents for settling troubling issues.

Drop the "victim" excuse. Clean up your side of the street first. I am a practicing Catholic. One form of prayer in the Catholic faith is an exercise called a "novena." A novena is a course of prayer that is coupled with attempting to perform some good works, performed for the resolution of a troubling problem.

Thirty years ago I made a novena, fervently praying for divine intervention in regard to a failing business venture. My thought, my opinion, was that the failure of the business was everyone's fault but mine. Vendors weren't fair, customers didn't pay invoices fast enough, my employees weren't trying hard enough—it was a conspiracy. Or so I thought. Or wanted to think.

Once I began the novena, things started to become a little, a lot, clearer to me. *I was the problem.* The exercises that the novena called for were extremely illuminating. Those exercises included "being kind to those to whom you feel aversion," "bridle your tongue," and "strive to amend your predominant fault," among others. A different exercise, like the ones above, was required each week for nine consecutive weeks. At the end of the novena it was clear that I was the sole designer of the whole mess I was in and I was the only one who could right the ship. *You* are responsible for your successes and your failures—even in this current era of denying and re-spinning the truth. Wanna be successful? Clean up your side of the street first.

Don't take it personally—take it professionally. When confronted with an upset customer you can't, and shouldn't, take it personally—even if you had nothing to do with the wrongdoing or mishandling of the situation. And … you can't take it personally even if you *are* the cause of the problem. Think about it this way. How many times have you found someone to be annoying, irritating, or in general having a gruff, unpleasant personality? Probably fairly often. How many times have you heard the "story behind the story" about one of those people and reacted with a healthy "Ohhhhhhhhhhhhhhhhhhhh," so that's why they act like that!" Usually the story behind the story is an enlightening tale about some horrible trouble or bad luck that scarred the person's personality. There's always a reason why people act like they act.

Enjoy the book *The five people you meet in heaven* by Mitch Albom. It will give you great relief and reassurance about the travails we all have behind the curtain and the importance of not prejudging. And it will give you a professional style without being distracted by your client's behavior. There's always a reason. It has nothing to do with you. Take it professionally.

Take the first step: self-management. There are three critical steps to creating a great organization. The first step is having a team of individuals who are interested and serious about self-management and constant improvement. Like never before, due largely to America's Customer Service Disaster, there is an opportunity to do what we all strive for—to create a great organization. To create a great team. Being part of a great team gives the individual and the organization the fortuitous, unique, and elusive boon in the business setting—*blurring the lines.*

Blurring the lines, in this context, means diminishing the often monolithic wall between work, home, and vacation. Twice in my business career, the lines between work, home, and vacation were nonexistent. Whether I was at work, at home, or on the beach with my family, my heart and mind were in the same comfortable place. Why? How? Because in all instances I was part of a great team, a great organization. It can be done. On the other hand, there have been times in my business career where the wall between work, home, and vacation was 100 feet high with snakes crawling all over it. For those of us in the wrong, un-blurred setting, the wall does a lot of growing on Sunday evening. The formula for creating a great team is easy to describe and difficult to accomplish. It requires three steps:

1. Find individuals who self-manage and strive to improve.
2. Once you have #1, you can build a team.
3. Once numbers 1 and 2 are complete, the external customer will knock the door down to do business with you.

Find YOUR key. Cluster your way to greatness. In his book *Peak Performance,* Dr. Charles Garfield describes a self-discovery exercise called "clustering." The point of the exercise is to find the unique key to one's volition, or self-determination. What's particularly enlightening about this exercise is that YOU find what technique or behavior works best for you. You are finding your own key in the clustering—it's not coming from a motivational speaker telling an audience of 500 people how to become successful by all using the exact same things. You find your own unique key in clustering. The clustering exercise gives an individual clarity on behavioral specifics that make things work for them, and the formula for their personal success.

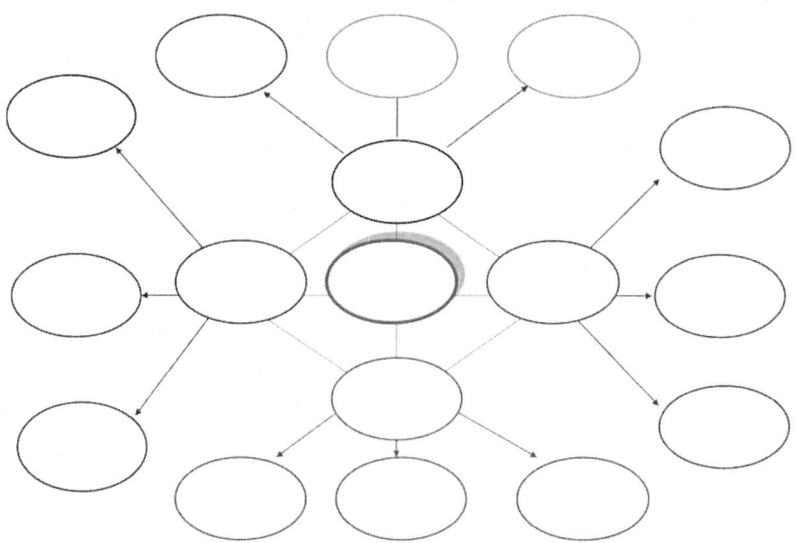

I found the keys in clustering I needed to invoke if I decided to embark on a new venture or get a wobbly one back on track. For me those keys are patience, preparation, and practice. All of those particular keys may come instinctively to some but not me. For me they are a struggle. BUT, when I apply those keys, good things happen.

Instructions

Pick an event or an accomplishment in which you performed extremely well. Something that gave you great joy, happiness, or exhilaration. It can be relevant to a personal relationship or business or a hobby or a sport—whatever. The key is to pick something you were/are great at—and everybody is great at something, even if it's cooking spaghetti!

Place the selected event/accomplishment in the center circle. Now begin to brainstorm about the items, issues, or behaviors that were the elements that brought your accomplishment to fruition. As they come to mind, note them in the circles emanating from the center circle that describes your accomplishment.

Continue with open, random, thinking until the "key" or "keys" to your success become evident.

CLUSTER EXERCISE

What is something that you've done in a GREAT, exceptional manner?

 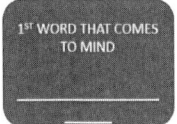 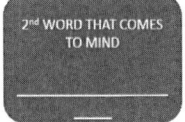 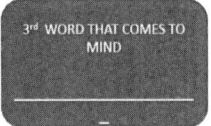

The author Marianne Williamson writes, "Our deepest fear is not that we are inadequate. Our deepest fear is that we are powerful beyond measure. It is our LIGHT, not our darkness, which most frightens us. We ask ourselves, 'who am I to be brilliant, talented and famous'? Your playing small doesn't serve the world. There's nothing enlightening about shrinking so that other people won't feel small around you. As we let our own light shine, we unconsciously give other people permission to do the same."

Wow. How strong are those words? How is it that this "shrinking" that Ms. Williamson refers to has become so comfortable, become such a haven for one's security? What has caused this? Is it the fear of failure or the fear of being ridiculed or criticized? Maybe it's one or the other or both. After all, like never before there now exists platforms for anonymous buffoons to ridicule the efforts of others without recourse. They do so under the guise of untraceable nicknames. A perfect storm for cowards. I subscribe to Ms. Williamson's theory that if you feel you have a special talent, a special gift, run with it. Don't be afraid to embrace and wear your gift proudly. As Albert Einstein put so eloquently, "Great spirits have always encountered violent opposition from mediocre minds."

Understand your importance. Front-line empowerment. If you are on the front line, meaning that you deal directly with customers, it is critical that you bearhug certain skills and techniques in our job. Like it or not, you, the person on the front line, are giving the most critical impression of your company and your organization. You are the cover of the book. You are the first, and sometimes only, impression made on the customer.

When you're on the front line, remember these points:

- Speak up. Talk clearly and distinctly. 95% of the time when we go through the fast food drive-thru lines, the attendees on the other end of the speaker can't be understood. Orders have to be repeated and the line backs up. And the food gets cold. And the customers get aggravated. And the customer doesn't come back—all because a little effort in speaking clearly is missing.

- If you are dealing with an irate customer, don't get into a word race with them! Don't try to outtalk the customer. See the "10 steps to correctly addressing a disgruntled customer" below to that follow. In the great majority of instances, the thing the troubled customer wants the most is to be heard. To get their ya-ya's out. Listen with the intent of understanding the problem. Then, solve the problem. If you can't solve the problem, give it to someone who can—and explain to the customer that you've handed their issue off to higher ground. Don't leave the customer confused.

- After those steps are taken, call the customer one extra time to make sure all is okay. If you don't take this last step, you have wasted your time. If you find you are constantly getting your head bashed in by the same types of complaints from customers over and over, tell management. If you are working for a sound, reputable company, they want to hear about your troubles and your ideas about how to resolve them. If you have problems doing any of this naturally—if you don't feel you are instinctive about taking care of an issue or disgruntled customer, lock on to this formula:

10 steps to correctly addressing a disgruntled customer

1. There are always going to be unhappy people. You can't change that fact. What you can change is how you react to it, which is a blessing that can make your workday more enjoyable.
2. Say "I am sorry" and mean it.
3. Let the customer get their ya ya's out. They want to empty out on someone. All you have to do is listen. All they want you to do is listen.
4. Don't try to win the race or win the argument. Just listen.
5. Listen with the intent of understanding.
6. Resolve the problem using your God-given talent.
7. If you can't resolve the problem, give it to someone who can (manager, trusted associated, HR, etc.)
8. After you have resolved the problem or handed it off, tell the customer what is going to happen next.
9. Apologize. This is not humbling yourself. It is correctly representing your company.
10. Finally. Call the customer back in a timeline consistent with your promise to have the problem addressed. If you do not take this final step, you have wasted all the effort you put into this.

Avoid the Dead Stare. Simply looking the customer in the eye will distinguish you from a lot of behavior in the marketplace. Lose the dead stare. Look the customer in the eye with the intent of helping as you speak clearly and respectfully. Brick-and-mortar stores are losing business every minute to the internet. There's a reason. In a lot of cases, doing business with a PC or tablet or smartphone is not only easier, *it's friendlier!* People are tired of disinterested attendants, even though the population of such is shooting through the stars.

Educate the team. Today, Learning Management Systems, the platform used to train and educate employees, is a 2.5 BILLION dollar industry. Companies may decide to manage their own LMS systems and the money is spent on wonderful tools, like the 7 Habits of Highly Effective People, Excel, and Time Management. Others may subscribe to LMS systems that bring the whole package of training and learning to work, like Cross Knowledge, Brainer, and Wisetail. Whatever the delivery system might be, people have to learn how to apply the training to their current position. It's not hard to find bank employees who are lacking in financial knowledge or librarians who don't read much. Or writers who can't write worth a damn, like me. Educate your team about what they are doing day to day.

Don't be afraid of failure. Embrace it! Failure is magical. Failure can bring you to your foundation and carve a path for the successes you've dreamed of. Failure can take you to the place where you're supposed to be. When I use the term "foundation," I do not mean bringing you down low or to the bottom. I mean starting from a foundation that can take you where you need to go.

If you want to be a juggler in the circus, and you're not a very good juggler, failure to master juggling will show where you need to improve or give you the clarity to see that what you really should be doing is running the Ferris Wheel. Think of it this way: Failure creates experience, experience creates knowledge, and knowledge creates wisdom. Therefore *failure creates wisdom.*

Great athletes get a million-dollar lesson when they make a bad play. They learn exactly how to do it better by virtue of their previous failing. Great writers and great filmmakers learn from past mistakes in a way that leads them to writing great books and creating award-winning films. Today we run from, deny, and are embarrassed by failure, when it truly serves as the best learning path. No one wants to make the same mistake twice, and they seldom do, because they have LEARNED from the first mistake. The successes I cherish most in my life, those that mean the most to me, have been the direct result of a previous failing. When you have a painful failure, learn from it. Don't run from it.

Closing thoughts to ponder regarding thin-skinned behavior

According to *USA Today*, the five most common personal behaviors that hurt the business setting are:

1. **Bringing stuff to work.** If you had a fight at home, leave it there.

2. **Becoming Mr. or Ms. Defensive.** If you can't embrace criticism, you're never going to be great at your job.

3. **Being nonresponsive.** We already talked about Gordon Matthews' invention, *voice mail.* Learn to use voice mail correctly, or answer the phone!

4. **Being lazy.** Put your back into it. Push a little. If you're getting a regular paycheck, that's the least you owe the one who signs the check.

5. **Engaging in "He said, she said."** Don't join the fellowship of the miserable. Stay away from the coffeepot crowd. Concentrate on getting better at your trade.

Thin Skinned Behavior IS CURED BY ▶ Self Management

Review

Solutions for thin-skinned behavior:

- Know who you are dealing with. Take the personality test.
- DROP the victim excuse. Clean up your side of the street first.
- Don't take it PERSONALLY. Take it PROFESSIONALLY.
- Self-manage. Get better at your trade. That will create confidence.
- Find YOUR key. Cluster your way to success.
- Understand your importance.
- Get rid of the Dead Stare. Look the customer in the eye.
- Educate yourself. If you don't know something, ask.
- Learn from the Magic of Failure.
- If you have trouble, just follow the 10 steps to handing a disgruntled customer.

Now you're ready to be part of a team. Now you're ready to be successful. Now the customer will seek you out.

Illustration by Steve Ford down at the Tollhouse

'The guy who has '_helped_' us. Time after time after time after time after time. In person _and_ over the phone.'

Chapter Three: The misuse of technology

With all the technology available today, all the technical weaponry and intelligence and power and skill that's in the marketplace, you would think we would use it to better connect to the external customer. In reality we have used it to *build a wall between the customer and the service provider.* And the wall is tough as hell to penetrate.

Misuse of technology is prevalent and maddening to the external customer in nearly every line of business. It is challenging to do the simplest things because of the misuse of technology. For example, see what happens if you want to change some item on a contract that includes you and your wife or husband. We are left trying to get our spouse conferenced in to a call with the service provider so a simple request can be acknowledged.

Here's one of my favorites. I'm on the phone (in itself a remarkable accomplishment) with the local cable provider. I am talking to the fourth person about my problem, one that finally is void of thin-skinned behavior and is really trying to help. We are making progress. I am informed by someone in my office that an important call—one that is critical and one that I've been waiting for—has come in on another line. I ask the helpful attendant if I can call her back directly and, in total embarrassment, she says, "I'm so sorry Mr. Karem, but you can't call me directly. You will have to go back through the main number." Go back through the main number. Go back through a cacophony of "customer hatred reps" and "managers" and "supervisors" until I get another person with the skills of my current helper. Who designs this crap? Is that really the best way to use all the technology available?

I've talked long and hard on previous pages about the effect of voice mail in the business setting. I don't think too much can be made of the disastrous manner in which voice mail is used. Imagine a scene in 1967 in the offices of an insurance company. Betty and Fred are at the coffeepot having a discussion about last Saturday's game. The phone rings. You can be sure that Betty AND Fred jump to answer the phone. If the same scene is played out today, in 2019, neither Betty nor Fred is going to answer the phone, even if they have Bluetooth connections on their ear. The conversation about the game on Saturday is going to be completed while the phone call goes into voice mail, regardless of the importance of the call. Is that a good use of technology?

Along with the misuse of voice mail you have the dreaded and obnoxious, but always present, use of needless and time-wasting recordings. One of these is "Please listen closely, as our menu options have changed." Does anyone really know the OLD menu options? Or "This call may be recorded for quality assurance purposes." Really? Has anyone in California, Oregon, Vermont, Tennessee, Delaware, or Alaska ever received a call back from a poorly handled call? I don't think so. And don't tell me that the recording is for internal use only, because if that's the case they really are missing the boat. Other examples of the misuse of technology include:

- Please continue to hold. Your call is very important to us.
- I'll need to speak to the primary cardholder.

Here are a few stories that illustrate the misuse of technology in our current business setting, and some solutions.

Stop the presses—someone used technology effectively!!!

Just when you've heard "Please listen closely, as our menu options have changed" or the dreaded "This call may be recorded for quality assurance purposes," someone FINALLY comes up with a way to use technology effectively!

A few weeks ago, I lost my wallet. Unfortunately, losing my wallet, cell phone, and keys has been a reoccurring theme for a long time—since solved by selecting the Tile app on my smartphone. Tile is a neat gadget for old geezers that all but eliminates losing stuff. You put a little chip on your keychain, another in your wallet, and download the app on your phone and your troubles are over. The chips make chirping noises when engaged so you can find your phone when it's down in the couch, and your keys when they're under the car seat.

Nonetheless, that wonderful invention is not what this story is about. This story occurred before I discovered the Tile solution to empty space in the brain. As stated, I lost my wallet, which carried my credit cards and all the other needed credentials. So, after losing all this stuff, I had to go through the usual gauntlet of canceling cards and ordering new ones. Getting my driver's license replaced was an easy trip to the county clerk's office, but getting new copies of my credit cards was a little tougher. After canceling the lost cards, I found this note on my front door:

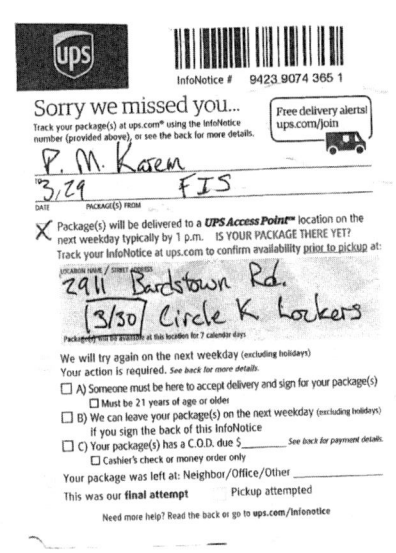

The note apprises me of a missed delivery attempt to my home and includes instructions to go to 2911 Bardstown Road to retrieve this mysterious item. I travel to the required destination, thinking all the while that it is going to be a UPS store. When I get to 2911 Bardstown Road, I'm upset because it's a Circle K gas station. What's happening? Did the UPS delivery person put the wrong address on the "We missed you" note? I go inside the Circle K to try to find out what is going on. I'm greeted by a young lady named

Shay, who has all the customer service skills she will ever need. Shay walks me around the side of the gas station and, lo and behold, there is a UPS kiosk, surrounded by about 40 small lockers. Shay gives me a short syllabus on how to operate this thing and here's what happened:

1. I put the UPS note (see previous page) in a scanner.
2. The scanner reads the UPS note and then …
3. A request comes up on the scanner screen telling me to scan my driver's license, the new one recently acquired.
4. The screen on the kiosk then reads "Your request is approved. Locker E-1 is now opening."
5. Damn if that ain't exactly what happened. And in locker E-1 is a UPS envelope with a newly replaced credit card.

What a great, convenient, effective use of technology, especially today, when technology often presents an impenetrable wall rather than an easy solution for consumers and customers.

Boy have the menu options changed! Thank goodness!

This story is recorded for quality assurance purposes.

Thank you UPS, thank you locker E-1, thank you Shay.

Here is another.

A story of a business owner answering the phone

If you've read any of the stories on my website or attended one of my speaking engagements or classes, you've heard me talk about how focusing on the customer and applying seemingly rudimentary customer service practices can distance your business from the competition.

Here is a perfect example of just that.

A close friend of mine was searching desperately for some wine he and some associates enjoyed while vacationing in France last year. My friend lives in Louisville, KY, and couldn't find any bottles of the desired brand in our area so he reached out to my daughter, JoAnna (who is in the wine business) to see if she could help him find this wine. The name of the wine was Chateau Tour des Gendres 2008," which, quite frankly, means nothing to yours truly as I am a wine idiot.

After doing some digging, JoAnna was able to find the wine at a place called Integrity Wines in Atlanta, GA. She provided me with the phone number, so I called to inquire about the wine.

I called the number given and this is how our conversation went.

"Hello, this is Doug."

"I'm sorry, Doug. I must have the wrong number. I was looking for Integrity Wines."

Who answers the phone anymore if they don't recognize the number these days?

Doug says, "Yes, I am the owner of Integrity Wines."

After I pick myself up off the floor and take a few breaths to prevent hyperventilation, I explain how I got his contact information and tell him what I'm looking for.

He is pleased with the referral and it turns out he has the wine in stock! Then the impossible happens. Doug says, "If you send me an email I will get this taken care of."

After Doug provides his email address, he says, "This might take a few days. I'm currently driving in the French countryside and it's raining cats and dogs!"

Mind blown.

Who would believe it? The owner of a business answering the phone and talking to a customer. Just when the founders of voice mail have extended the extra recording after the personal message by two extra minutes, just when the authors of voice mail have successfully imbedded non-answering of the phone by business owners and managers into the United States Constitution, and just when 45-minute holds have become the norm, a business owner answers the phone! On a different continent. On his cell phone. In the middle of a rainstorm!

There you have it. Just the way business is supposed to, and used to, work; courteous people helping each other. Not being annoyed with a phone call but seeing the phone call as an opportunity. AND, Doug answered the phone in France, where most AT&T, Sprint, and Mobile One users visiting from America would have a heart attack from the forthcoming charges—certain to be more than the "special" plan for the trip.

Not only does Doug have a customer for life in my friend, but who do you think my friend is going to contact the next time he's looking for a special bottle of wine? Better yet, who do you think my buddy is going to refer his friends to the next time they're searching for wine that's not sold in their location?

- Voice Mail Police: 0
- Doug at Integrity Wines: 1 (and … many dollars; probably enough to pay the phone bill)

A story of tech gone awry

Here is a personal example of the horrid misuse of technology. Once, my wife and I decided to take the daring and terrifying step of switching our cable and internet services to another provider. We had had enough of the issues with Spectrum and decided to flip our enlistment over to AT&T/ DirecTV. This opportunity came to us through a door-to-door call from a courteous, well-mannered, and well-intended young man who convinced us that the AT&T customer service would be consistent with his splendid style. We were wrong.

After signing up for the new service, we were scheduled for the installation crew to arrive at our home and perform the install. The designated time of arrival was scheduled between 9 and 11 am. Two days prior to the installation, my wife called AT&T/DirecTV to get some basic questions answered. A recording told her that her expected hold time was "less than one minute." Twenty-six minutes later, *26*, she finally had a customer hatred rep on the phone. Strike One. My wife's efforts to change all the contact information from my cell and email to hers, which was the intent of her call, were left unattended and unchanged, as I continued to get annoying emails and texts the next day. Strike Two.

The day of the installation I—again me, not my wife—got a text notifying me that the time of arrival for the installation team would be "sometime after 11am." Strike Three. We cancelled the install. While canceling the install, the attendant, upon hearing our notice of cancellation, said, "I don't blame you." Even a savings of $150+ per month over the disastrous service of Spectrum was not enough to go through all this. And if the service was this frustrating before installation, just imagine what it would be like after the install was completed.

With all the talent and technology it has, AT&T just fell into the same customer service swamp most businesses today dwell in. With all that skill and technology to their avail, look how they used it. The day we canceled the installation, AFTER we canceled by text and phone recording, we still received yet another call from the install crew informing us of their arrival time. When we received a follow-up call from the impressive young man who enrolled us in this adventure, it hurt us to inform him that his efforts went for naught.

Today, AT&T has television ads that are hypnotic and sweep you off your feet. One claims a product that is "unlimited," "unbelievable," and "unreal." Another says AT&T is our "only hope." Well, my only hope was that I could get AT&T service in our home and save $150.00 a month, but alas, it could not be done. One would think an "unlimited" and "unbelievable" and "unreal" company could hook up service, on time, in a residential home. I have to give AT&T the hat trick—that being, accomplishing each of the three hallmarks of America's Customer Service Disaster:

- **Thin-skinned behavior:** How? We canceled the installation, after two days of nonsense, and the technician's response was, "I don't blame you."
- **Misuse of technology:** Where do I start? With all the technical muscle AT&T has, it can't return phone calls, correct email contacts, or coordinate appointments.
- **The Disconnect:** After the experience we had, as we watch AT&T's self-praising media ads, you have to wonder if it has any idea how silly it appears.

That is the customer service environment of today. Wow. What an opportunity! What a chance to take a quantum leap in securing customers and building the brand and image of a company.

Solutions

Act Like Ed. Ed Manassah is executive director, Institute for Media, Culture and Ethics, at Bellarmine University in Louisville, KY. He is a retired publisher of the *Louisville Courier Journal* (1993-2006). He served in leadership positions from city editor to publisher at six Gannett Co., Inc., newspapers beginning in 1972. He was on the *USA Today* startup team in 1982. Upon his retirement from *The Courier Journal*, Ed designed the curriculum, syllabus, and entire concept behind the Institute for Media. A talented, gifted, generous, and BUSY man.

I emphasize "busy" for this reason: During his career, and you can only imagine how busy the career of a publisher of a major newspaper could be, Ed Manassah took his phone with him—and answered it—regardless of where he was or what he was doing. He took it on vacation, to meetings, and while driving (Bluetooth for safety), traveling, working out, and eating. He was married to his phone for professional reasons—those reasons being internal and external customer service excellence. He used his cell phone, a remarkable but terribly misused piece of our technology, as a "weapon" to connect to and respect employees, adversaries, family, and associates, and to take critical calls.

I use the term "weapon" here in the positive sense—as a means of contending with the course of the business day. He used it to deal quickly with employee issues and concerns, civic problems that needed addressing by the city's only major newspaper, contentious issues that required fast resolution, union problems, non-union problems, and all the other items that called for urgent action from someone managing a public trust.

Ed Manassah used the telephone in a manner that is rare and absent in today's business environment. He used it as a business weapon. Guess what? That opportunity, the opportunity to use the phone as a business tool, a business weapon, is available to anybody today. And in using the phone in that manner, just as Ed did, you will distinguish yourself from the competition. If you don't think so, consider this: How many times have you made an important call to a voice mail recording? No answer. So you leave a voice message. And to emphasize the point, consider further: How many times has that same voice message gone unanswered and unrecognized? Today, calls are not only not answered, they are not even returned in a courteous, timely manner. Want a new business weapon? Act Like Ed.

Let the customer set the pace. When I graduated from college I was not prepared to enter the world of work. One reason was that I was spoiled. I had the good fortune to attend the University of Kentucky on a football scholarship. One of the many benefits of an SEC grant-in-aid is the support one receives getting through the challenges of college life.

We didn't have to go through registering for classes like the other students—it was done for us. We didn't eat the same cafeteria food the other students ate—we had a training table with a humongous selection, right in front of the other, starving students. Trouble with a class? No problem. Just huddle up with one of the many tutors available to the team every evening. Trouble parking your car? Again, no problem. Just pick up your permit specially created for parking next to the football dorm. All this contributed to spoiling us and making the jump from college athlete to entry-level worker a little sketchy for most has-beens.

Somehow, some way, I landed in the mortgage business after college. Still not sure how that happened, but the mortgage business has been awfully good to me over the years, and for a lot of those years I traveled on the wings of others. I was blessed to learn from some of the best in the business. One particular lesson still resonates with me and I fear it is a lesson lost with a lot of people.

At the very outset of my mortgage career I was employed by Churchill Mortgage, an Atlanta company with branches all over the South. The northern outpost of Churchill Mortgage was in Louisville. I was a plebe mortgage originator, running around like a chicken with my head cut off, selling FHA and VA home financing.

I was a little slow on the draw in reacting to customers, and our regional manager, a classy gentleman named Bill Manning, picked that up right away. One evening, Bill came to town and took the five or six of us in the branch out to dinner. I remember Bill instructing the waiter, upon being served the wine Bill had ordered, to "Let it breathe." I had no idea what the hell that meant, but I was swept away with how cool our regional manager was. After dinner and drinks (we are talking about 1978, when drinking and eating on the company was a big, bigger than today, part of business), Bill congratulated the team on a stellar year and expressed hopes that the rookie, me, would soon join in the success.

Bolstered by my first, second, and third martinis, I decided to wrench the tricks of the trade from my cool regional manager. So I asked Mr. Manning how it was that he became so successful and what were the keys to this business. I clearly remember Mr. Manning looking me in the eye and saying, "I never let a call go unanswered for more than 30 minutes." Knocked me back a little. Knocked the spoiled athlete right out of me. You have to realize that in 1978, there were no cell phones, no texting, no voice mail or instant messaging, and "recording" machines were barely on the scene. And the recording machines were at the office and no calls went to those machines during office hours. None. So, anxious to defend my slow response habits and still under the spell of the spoiled athlete who had everything done by others, I asked an important question: "Bill, I am out calling on realtors all day long. If I am going to respond to every call in 30 minutes or less, where am I going to call from?"

His response jerked a knot in my brain. He said, "Call from a phone." In other words, get off your behind and figure out a way. Borrow the realtor's phone or go to a payphone at the grocery store, or whatever! He said it with just the perfect inflection and emphasis to embarrass me in front of the big producers. The point was this. Find a way to call the office and get your messages. If you don't call the customer back promptly (which in those days was 30 minutes or less), the prospective customer is going to call someone else. It hit me like a rock in the forehead. The easy days were over and it was time to perform.

Today, 30 minutes is an eternity. Today, you can return a call while driving a car just by telling the phone to "Call Ed." But today, amazingly, those calls are not returned as fast as they were in 1978. Today, a lot of business calls are not even returned. Today, that blinking red light indicating a voice message is often not even engaged in the same day. It is technology mis-used and a lack of respecting the urgency that might be the reason for the call. Voice mail is setting the pace, not the customer.

Bill Manning looked like the coolest guy in the world in this three-piece suit, pastel tie, and instructions to the waiter to "Let it breathe." Honestly, today, and since that dinner, I have trouble breathing easily if I have unre-turned phone calls.

Your competition sets its own pace for how it returns phone calls or texts or emails from customers.

Try this: Let the customer set the pace!

Received a bad customer service review? Great! No question about it. When you receive a bad customer service review, it stings. Especially when you tried so hard and thought you performed better than you really did. But even with a bad review, the good far, far, outweighs the bad.

First of all, making the effort to get the real story about customer experience from your clients is critical to the success of any business. Making the effort to hear what your customers have to say is in itself a distinguishing element because few businesses really make the effort in an effective manner. Presenting the customers' service reviews or evaluations in the most provoking, effective manner is what separates getting true feedback from customers from getting lip service.

Using the most effective vernacular, such as "Help us improve our performance" or "Thank you for your business; please tell us how we could have served you better," may be just the medicine that can get the real story from a hesitant customer. I do not see that kind of dialogue coming from big companies that rely on automated, and misused, technology to glean honest customer reviews. It appears that they aren't really trying. Maybe they're afraid of bad news. In today's business setting, bad news may be the best coaching or business advice available. All the customer is trying to do is help you get better at your trade. Turning away from tough criticism is a chance missed to take a quantam leap in performance.

Look at the success of Domino's pizza. Once reputed to be serving "cardboard with ketchup on top," Domino's took a deep dive into the impressions of the customer and found a way to excite the entire team about doing something to correct its bad image.

In the *Harvard Business Review*, Bill Taylor described the turnaround this way: "Leaders who want to shake things up have to be comfortable with the idea that 'failure *is* an option,'" he said, quoting Domino's CEO Patrick Doyle. "In a world of hyper-competition and nonstop disruption, playing it safe is the riskiest course of all. That's a recipe for reinvention that makes for good pizza and big change." And you can bet the better recipe for reinvention comes from your customers.

Possibly a more frightening aspect, and an additional call to action regarding customer service reviews, is that 96% of those experiencing bad or subpar customer service *won't even tell you about it.* But what they will do is tell 15 or more people about the experience they've endured. And for more good news and fun, consider the fact that those 15 people, having heard the bad story, will each tell three to five more. If you do the math you can see that one terrible customer service experience can generate 90 people who hear about the trouble first hand. And those numbers are changing as you are reading them. Facebook, Twitter, Yelp, Foursquare, The Better Business Bureau, Expresit, Glassdoor, Google Reviews, and Home Advisor are all sites where thousands of people can hear about the bad job a company or individual performed.

The point is this: If you do a bad job, the customers, the consumers, already know about it. The public already knows what kind of job you do. So you'd better lean into it and do something about it. Better yet, make gleaning honest reviews from your customers part of your everyday business model. As much as anything, it will show you the path to the success you seek.

Do all you can to find the REAL impressions of your customers.

It's the FAST LANE to success.

Respond to bad reviews personally. One of the least effective uses of technology today is engaging the internet, or chat, or whatever kind of technical dialogue, to resolve a customer complaint. We've all been through this.

So there you have yet another example of the failings of technology. Something that is waiting to be used in a positive, effective, time-saving, reputation-saving manner is doing just the opposite—and frustrating the daylights out of people at the same time. Funny how the companies that have their customer service efforts steadfast in the main category—thin-skinned behavior—also seem to have it right in all the other spots. For example, Southwest, my favorite airline by far, has timely flights coordinated by helpful, personable staff, and it has the most user-friendly website. The point is this: Technology will never be used in the best interest of customer service if the designers of that same technology have no clue about the customer service issues they are trying to resolve.

Use the live chats and customer service reviews you receive to seek out the unpleasant customer reviews and then:

Respond personally.

Dear Annie: Customer service sparks frustration

Dear Annie: Am I the only one who feels that life is too complicated these days and that I feel absolutely powerless when it comes to calling a big company to get service? I am old enough to remember the days when we bought a television, put it in the car, drove home, plugged it in, played with the "rabbit ears" for a minute and then were able to watch TV.

Today, when you buy a television, it is a major project. If it's a big-screen TV, someone usually has to deliver it, and then you need to make an appointment with an installer. It always takes much longer for them to install than they plan.

Then there is the cable company. This morning I waited for over an hour for the cable guy to arrive. After working on the TV for more than an hour, he said he had the wrong parts and box and needed to go back to his office to get new supplies.

My wife had made lunch for me, but I told her to wait until this guy was finished. Then, after he left to get the new parts, we got a chance to eat, though we were both watching the clock.

Two hours later, the man returned and, after another hour, finally got everything set up.

Of course, I appreciate that the television quality and choice of channels are a million times better than those days of rabbit ears, but I feel so frustrated by the feeling of powerlessness I have if something goes wrong. You may as well call the federal government in terms of not getting a person. They have one recording after another, push this button or that, stay on hold for 20 minutes, and then maybe, if you are lucky, you will be able to talk to a live human.

The airlines are the same way. I remember the old days when I would call an airline, someone would answer the phone, book my flight or whatever, and we would both be on our way. Now, in the "new and improved" technological society, there is never any personal customer service. Everything is automated and impersonal.

While we have had improvements because of technology, we have had regression in terms of customer service and personal attention.

I started writing this letter out of frustration with our cable company, but the more that I wrote, the angrier I got in thinking about how impersonal business has become. You always are the voice of common sense, and I'm wondering if you have any suggestions. -- *Helpless and Powerless*

Dear Helpless and Powerless: Help is on the way, and it is coming in the shape of you discovering your own power. While you might not have the power to fix your television immediately, you do have the power to change your perspective. You were able to have a pleasant, quiet and electronic-free lunch with your wife. Time without TV can sometimes be a nice break.

However, I agree with you that automated "customer service" is a contradiction in terms, though it has become common practice today. Customer service should be all about the customer feeling respected and heard. You are not alone in your frustrations.

We have seen many incredible advances because of modern technology, but the same cannot be said about typical customer service. Imagine if a company could offer the efficiencies of modern improvements with Marshall Field's old maxim from more than a century ago, "The customer is always right." The companies that can manage both are the ones that will emerge as victors in the future.

Try the intranet answer. A well-designed intranet can solve a lot of technical and behavioral problems for a company and solve a lot of customer service issues at the same time. I marvel at the experience of traveling to an AT&T store. Unfailingly, the small box stores, maybe 1,500 square feet, have the walls lined with posters depicting scenes of blissful customers. Everybody depicted in the posters is thrilled and smiling. A nice elderly lady is smiling while chatting on the phone. A handsome young lad is texting with glee. A college coed is connecting via cell to her class schedule. All of these scenes are depicted with everybody included—even a golden retriever running along next to his cell phone-operating-while-jogging owner.

But the scene in the store is drastically different. There are always at least 10 to 12 customers in the store, waiting impatiently for the "next available attendant." All the customers are mad and all the attendants are mad as well. The customers are mad because they are either having trouble with the cell phone or with the cell phone bill. They are in no way similar to the smiling people on the all-encompassing posters because they are MAD.

Guess what? The attendants are mad because they know they are not going

Illustration by Steve Ford down at the Tollhouse

to be able to help most of the waiting, angry customers. They know this because all the disgruntled customers who come in the store day after day after day have the same problems and the same issues—and the attendants have to give a lot of them the same answer: "Sorry, I can't help you."

In an industry that just might have the largest profit gap existent in business, I marvel at the lack of support the downtrodden attendants are saddled with. With the same problems surfacing day after day after day, why in the world aren't the attendants authorized to do simple things like give a customer a $25.00 credit for enduring some fashion of misery? Without fail, I see the attendants turning away a frustrated customer with a considerable increase in frustration. All because simple issues aren't resolved.

Wouldn't an effective intranet system solve a lot of these issues? Wouldn't a guide or primer on solving simple mistakes make the people in the store smile like the people on the posters? A well put together intranet guide would work wonders for the reputation of the company and abort the ongoing dynamic created when an unhappy customer tells all who will listen about their bad experience. Especially when the problems that arrive at the front door are the same ones over and over and over.

The point is this: Since the problems are repetitive, solutions can be repetitive as well. Use the wonderful technology of an intranet platform as a guide, a "guard rail," for giving resolution to these reoccurring problems. Customers will be pleased and happy and so will the team—which is the real magic to customer service greatness. This applies to any industry out there, not just cell phone providers. Solve the problems before they arrive. Use the wonderful advances of technology effectively. Don't use the wonderful advances of technology to "Listen closely, as our menu options have changed."

Use the inTRAnet to HELP the team ... AND the customer.

Review

Solutions for misuse of technology:

- Be Like Ed—answer the phone!
- Respect the pace of the customer, not your pace.
- Remember that bad customer service reviews = business magic.
- Respond personally.
- Use the inTRAnet to solve repetitive issues.

Chapter Four: The Disconnect

The third piece of America's Customer Service Disaster is the Disconnect. The Disconnect is the gap between the claims service and goods providers make about their performance, as compared to the wide variance in the manner that those goods and services are delivered. The Disconnect in media advertising has hit near comedic levels. Some of the very worst service and goods providers have latched onto the idea that self-praising, self-laudatory advertising is the most effective strategy. The truth is that this methodology, designed to sweep customers off their feet with elaborate claims and self-praise, falls on deaf ears and a blind eye. Why? Because the customers already know what kind of job these companies do. The customer already knows the level of service these perpetrators of the Disconnect provide. Effusive self-praise isn't going to fool anybody anymore, with the advent of Yelp and all the other customer review sites, and the effect of word of mouth in the instance of repetitive bad customer service.

The haughty voice of Donald Sutherland is never going to get me on another Delta flight, and the AT&T claims of making "unbelievable" technological advances were not enough to switch my household over to AT&T from Spectrum, given the mess prior to installation. Advertising alone, especially in the face of bad performance, isn't going to fool anybody—not without performance that matches the claims.

Here are a couple of stories that illustrate the presence of the Disconnect in our current business setting, along with some solutions.

The world's greatest advertising campaign. probably right outside your door!

We all need advertising to promote or sell products and services. Advertising can be the greatest thing for your business or it can be an absolute bust. It all depends on the campaign and how and who is delivering it. Both scenarios happen every day. Even advertising agencies need to advertise, because just like all other businesses, it's essential for them to attract potential customers. As you have read above, or heard in one of our seminars, one of the critical pieces of America's Customer Service Disaster is the Disconnect in advertising claims today.

It is not difficult to find the Disconnect—it's EVERYWHERE! There are disconnects in advertising for air travel, fast food, hospitality, banking, insurance, cable services, cellular phone service, and just about every other category of business.

I have a theory about the comprehensive state of the Disconnect. Simply put, I think it happens because the company likes a jingle or pitch from the ad agency. And because the pitch is kind of cute and snappy, it's chosen to represent the company even though the ad does not accurately portray the way the company actually does business.

Recently, we had a problem with our cable provider—the same cable company whose ads all but claim it invented cable television and the internet. It could not be more self-laudatory. But with all its technology, all its weaponry, all its brains and machinery, all the company has really done is build a wall between the customer and what it provides—especially when the customer needs help.

You have to ask yourself, wouldn't the company be better served if it took the tack that Domino's Pizza took? Something along the lines of "We've listened to YOU, the customer, and here's what we are going to do about it!" Domino's turned its company and image around in one fell swoop by listening to its customers. If you need an edgy, shrewd ad campaign, then just send out some customer service evaluations to your customer base and they'll write the best ad campaign you'll ever find. You're not going to fool your customers with a catchy, clever ad. They already know exactly what kind of job you do.

As said in the fantastic book *Speak Human*:

"Let's suppose that your goal is to get people to love your brand. Consider some of the players and what their objectives might be. You, as the owner of the company (assuming you are this person) likely care the most about succeeding. Of all those involved, you have the most to gain but you're likely distracted by a number of things. Perhaps you're concerned about not going over budget. Maybe you have doubts about the ideas presented and want to hold on to the idea your buddy suggested. Alternately, you could be fighting with a supplier and finding it difficult to concentrate on any of this."

Instead of trying to digest all the complexities, like the issues above, the answer to how to pitch your company is right outside your door. There are two groups out there that can tell you EXACTLY what you need to say to the customers you want to attract:

- Your customers
- Your employees

The best ad people in the world.

And here is another story that illustrates the point even better.

Domino's pizza... what an exotic, radical way to turn a business around

If you order pizza on a regular basis, you're probably familiar with the story of Domino's' epic turnaround of a few years ago. For those of you who might not be familiar with it, here's a quick review.

It seems as though this company went from delivering cardboard covered with tomato sauce, stuck to the delivery box, to delivering delicious pizza with good cheese and tasty add-ons. On time. Easily ordered. How did this happen? Turns out it was an exotic, radical strategy—something completely contrary to the modern strategies that are formed by C-suite geniuses with MBAs and PhDs.

This risky gamble somehow has paid off, and nobody seems to understand why. Domino's has opened 1,800 new stores in 10 countries since this dramatic flip of the switch.

How did it do this?

Many will not understand this at first blush because it just doesn't make sense in today's customer service environment:

- Great personal attention and behavior by phone attendants
- Using technology in the best way to aid the customer in ordering
- Admitting the error of their ways and reacting to it

Domino's attacked and beat the three pieces of America's Customer Service Disaster: no thin-skinned behavior, no misuse of technology, and no advertising Disconnect.

Radical. Risky. Exotic.

Instead of arguing with customers, it listened to them. Rather than forming technology based on internal issues, Domino's formed it based on customer issues. It listened to the story of its misteps and reacted to it.

Here is what Erin Leedy of FRESHMR wrote about this remarkable turn-around:

"Listening to—and acting on—Social Media Feedback. A huge part of Domino's turnaround strategy was to listen to customer feedback and respond by making the needed changes to the taste and quality of the food."

Radical. Risky. Exotic.

- How could Domino's do this without having attendants become insulted with customer complaints?
- How could it do this without offering technology that made ordering a pizza possible only for IT geniuses, like the ones at Louisville Geek?
- How could it do this without producing self-praising, self-laudatory TV ads that were the exact opposite of how it was really performing at the time?
- Isn't that the way you are supposed to do things? Like all the other large companies?

LISTENING TO THE CUSTOMER.

RADICAL.

Solutions

Listen to your customers and to your team. One of the exercises included in the seminars we conduct goes like this. We usually have 12 to 15 attendees per event. During the section of the seminar dedicated to the Disconnect, we break the group up into four smaller groups. We ask each group to select a spokesperson and to select a company that is an example of the Disconnect—a company that delivers terrible customer service but claims just the opposite in its media advertising. Then we have the spokesperson from each group deliver a new advertising campaign for the selected company.

In many instances, the new ad campaigns that are proposed are eye-opening, entertaining, and the perfect antidote for the previous, deeply flawed ads that the disconnected company presents. And sometimes funny as hell. Most of the time, each group picks the same companies. The remedial media ads they come up with are spot on in regard to what these companies should be throwing at the consumer public.

Often chosen is a national cable provider with notoriously disconnected service reps and media ads that claim the opposite. We have had proposals in our seminars for this company that include daily rebates for any downtime in service, adjustments on invoices for tardy service calls, and dedication of a customer service rep for each household with an email address and a direct phone line. Absolute magic for an industry that drives people nuts!

Another subject that has been selected multiple times as a Disconnect target is an attorney in our region who has ads that suggest that all lawsuits are trips to instant wealth. The class exercise calls for the presenter to wear a coat and tie (to mimic the appearance of the attorney in his ads) and to give a little less assurance that every single lawsuit has the same return as a winning Powerball ticket. The reoccurring theme with all of these creative suggestions is to just tell the customer the truth.

Don't confuse your customer base. A lot of media ads try to cram 4,786 bits of information and every imaginable disclosure and disclaimer into a 60-second ad. Why? Where did this methodology come from? Are we so driven by the remote possibility of a lawsuit that we try to cover it all in 60 seconds? All this does is confuse the customer.

The typical rebuttal I get from some companies that advertise this way is that in our current, litigious society, everything has to be addressed. But it is so ineffective in the manner of address it really isn't going to make any difference anyway. Lots of these ads have so many words crammed into such few seconds that no one is going to pick it all up anyway.

Slow down and give the customer a succinct and honest message. The shorter the message, the more likely chance that the message will be heard. Look at the current trend in "less is more" advertising. Companies seek to scrunch down their names as their business reputations grow. The once iconic bookseller Borders went from Borders Bookstore to Borders Books to Borders. Right here in the Bluegrass state, Kentucky Fried Chicken got chewed down to KFC. Less is more. Make your point without confusing people.

Don't try to fool the customer. They already know what kind of job you do. For years and years and years, as the advent of bank takeovers and mergers thrived, each time a bank sold or merged, the media ad catchphrase was *New name, same great service.* We heard this message over and over. Problem was, and is, when there is a takeover, a disruptive period always follows and must follow—the settling of the nuances of the takeover.

Expenses are deduped. Locations are shut down if the purchasing bank (or whatever business) has a legacy location nearby. Executives and bean counters representing the takeover bank are sure to ask questions like "Do we really need all these people"? Decisions are going to be made in different locations—meaning you might not be able to just dial up "Fred" anymore to get a quick, direct answer like you used to. And on top of all this turmoil there is certain to be a strong move to centralize a lot of operations.

With all this going on, it is just not the time to tell people you've got a

New name, same great service. Without fail, these mergers always take customer casualties. Why not give the customer a different message so the expectations are a little more alerting? Why not tell the customer "Some changes are going to be made, and we may have a little turbulence in the next six months or so, but please stick with us and know that we have your satisfaction in mind." Why not set up a hotline or some phone base for people who get particularly confused or annoyed with the takeover confusion? Bottom line: You can't fool the customer.

Don't expect ad agencies to be the answer. No one can tell the story of your business like the people who are involved in it. Those include your team, your partners, your vendors, and your customers. They know your business and they know how it works. This is the piece that seems to be missing in ads designed by the modern ad agency. The self-laudatory style we referred to in the previous section seem to be the formula for the design of modern media ads. Everybody has jumped on this bandwagon and, as stated above, sometimes the bandwagon looks ridiculous.

Consider the *Business Insider* article of June 18, 2017, titled "The future of ad agencies has never been more in doubt." This article expounds on exactly what we are talking about—the need to tell your story earnestly and correctly to the buying public. To do so, the story has to be told by people who know your company. Who know what your company is about, what you stand for, and how you do things. If you are at a stage where you are not doing things so well, the last thing you want to say in a media ad is how terrific you are!

In the *Business Insider* article referred to above, the story is told of how Booking.com, a hotel e-commerce site owned by Priceline, decided to go internal for its media ads—both in placement and creation. Rather than spend millions of dollars to have an agency write catchphrases telling wonderful stories about Booking.com—which might not be exactly accurate—the company decided to do that internally. In some instances, simply listening to your customers might give you the best story to tell. For instance, Domino's, one of the best company/business turnarounds in history, simply listened to its customers, who said, "You are serving us cardboard with ketchup on top." The results speak for themselves. Bottom line: An outside entity better know as much about your company as your people do if they are going to craft a pitch or media ad.

Look to your employees and your customers for solutions. When you need an answer for problems bubbling up in your business or career, the best answer might be sitting right next to you. Imagine the synergy and team that could be created in the business setting if there were an exchange between co-workers about each other's' performance without causing an explosion of emotions. Imagine the synergy and team that could be built if warring parties inside the company could trade jobs for a month and get an idea of what the "other guy" has to deal with—and just maybe get an idea of how to do things a little better.

These exercises have been evicted from the business setting by virtue of the thin-skinned behavior piece of America's Customer Service Disaster. The fact of the matter is that no one knows what kind of job you do, and the keys to improving it, like the people you work with each and every day. Everyone strives to be a champion—to be great at their job—but a smaller number strive to go through the pain and effort it takes to create a great team.

Consider this: Think about professional sports teams for a moment. Do you really believe that the talent levels of the teams that are World Champions and the teams that finish way behind are widely different? Do you believe World Champions wear that crown because they are simply more talented than their competitors?

Well, here is a fact to consider while pondering those questions. Of every 10,000 high school seniors playing football, nine, NINE, become professional football players. Things are actually tougher in basketball, where three of every 10,000 high school senior basketball players make it to the pros. The same kinds of numbers prevail in ice hockey, women's basketball, soccer, and all other professional team sports. If the elite of the elite of the elite are the ones making it to the professional level, it stands to reason that the talent levels of these teams are only fractionally different, if at all. So what makes the championship teams thrive and teams like the Cleveland Browns finish last?

The answer is a word in the sentence in which the question is asked … and that word is *team*. The team element that the frustrated contenders are missing is learning from mistakes and learning from one another. I can personally attest to behavior on losing teams where it is verboten to offer constructive criticism of another team member because of the offensive manner in which the criticism is received. On the other hand, champions grab and crawl and snatch and slash and reach and nearly beg for feedback from coaches and fellow players about how to improve their craft, how to get better. They thirst for it continually and the results are trophies and locker rooms full of happy tears and void of sad tears.

What a great formula for business success—especially today during America's Customer Service Disaster. Let your competitors develop thin skin while your team lets helpful criticism and suggestions become a regular part of the "flow" of your business. Bottom line: The formula for your success is all around you. Reach out to your teammates for the truth about your performance.

Chapter Five: Internal customer service

As discussed previously, the three components and steps to building a great organization are:

1. Assembling a group of people who are self-managing and constantly self-improving
2. Unifying those parts unified into a team
3. If numbers 1 and 2 are done correctly, the external customer will knock the door down to do business with you.

Why? Because they are starving for the opportunity to deal with that kind of an organization. Starving. The second step in the critical path is often tough to accomplish and that's another reason why providers of customer service excellence are so rare.

Here are stories that illustrate flawed internal customer service in our current business setting, and some solutions.

Signs, signs, everywhere a sign

Look around at your workplace.

Take a good look at the signs, especially if they are intended reading for your external customers. I notice a lot of signs that are almost insulting to the customer. Most of those are in the doctor's office, although I must admit my personal doctor has no such signs and is very sensitive to exemplary customer service. He referred me to a specialist once, and the signs in that office gave me a further appreciation for my doctor. Here is what they said:

Takeaways

- Don't insult people you want to do business with.
- Don't insult your loyal, existing customers.
- Be aware that sometimes a sign on the outside is a hint of what's on the inside.

Best to watch out for the signs in your office. Might be a "SIGN" of bad customer service!!

And here is another story that illustrates the effect of bad internal customer service.

Employee turnover: Very costly—but there's a solution!

Man, it hurts to lose a good employee, a good teammate. On rare occasions, it's not so bad to see certain co-workers take a hike. But for the most part, it can be disruptive, hurtful, confusing, and most of all, expensive. It is hard to quantify the cost of employee turnover, but the Society of Human Resource Management takes a shot at it. Here is what SHRM says about the cost of losing an employee:

Every time a business replaces a salaried employee, it costs six to nine months' salary on average.

Six to nine months of salary on average.

Let's do the math on those numbers. Let's say you have a salaried mid-manager making $60,000.00 a year. You lose her. She was making $5K per month. The cost of replacing her, if you CAN replace her, is nine months. That's $45,000.00 going out the window for someone who is not even present in the building.

That number reflects the hidden costs of recruiting as well as new training for the replacement, placing the new hire into the company's learning management system (LMS), and the time it takes for the new hire to ramp up to the level of their predecessor's performance. Seems like it would make a lot of sense to try like the devil to lose as few people as possible.

Seems like companies would look long and hard into solutions for losing key people. If you've read *The Dream Manager* by Matthew Kelly, you're familiar with myriad ways to reach out to your team to discover what critical issues keep them engaged. I would strongly encourage you to read Mr. Kelly's book if you manage or own a business.

Why do people change jobs?

According to the *Harvard Business Review*, these are the main reasons:

- They don't feel valued.
- They don't see the organization as a place to succeed.
- They feel overworked.
- They feel that their opinions are without value—that they won't be heard.
- They do not feel appreciated.
- They feel they are treated unfairly compared to others.
- Their work lacks purpose.
- They don't see a career path.
- They have lost faith in the leadership.

Most of these people have been at the job for five years or more. How is it that they were lost?

Each of the reasons above falls into one category—internal customer service. And all of the reasons for employee loss are remedied with caring and communication. When we realize that people are our greatest asset, that's when management will find out about these issues before they happen. Tell someone how well they've done, and they'll feel valued. Tell someone how they can move upward in their job and they'll be motivated. Ask someone if they feel overworked and they will see that you care. Ask an employee their opinions about things and you will make them feel appreciated and important. Ask them if they understand the importance of what they are doing—and if they don't, tell them.

Ask them.

It's called *internal customer service.*

It's also called employee RETENTION.

Those are some bad, but often present, elements of poor internal customer service that we often deal with. Here are some solutions.

Turn vacations into real vacations! Folks love, love to go on vacation. Sometimes just to get away and sometimes to get the hell away. It is important for all of us to recharge and reboot when we are on vacation, and it is the business of the employer to see to it that the vacation works its magic. How do we do that? Well here is one antidote for making sure vacation time is not wasted: When someone goes on vacation, ensure that they do not come back to a mess. Make sure that the desk of the vacationer, and the problems left behind on the desk of the vacationer, and the lingering annoyances of the vacationer, are gone when the vacationer returns. This accomplished a number of positives:

1. The returning teammate does not come back to a mess. When someone comes back from vacation and walks into a big mess and lots of problems, the rest and reboot and freshness from the vaca-

tion are gone in seconds. The vacation is wasted. The returning vacationer is almost immediately drawn back into the "another hell day at work" syndrome. The vacation is *wasted.*

2. When your teammate returns to a hell hole, they're not alone—all of the other people in the office feel it! The dread and frustration of a nearby co-worker is hard to miss, and it is an infectious condition. It affects the others in the office and can frequently embarrass them with the realization that they let their buddy down— that they could have done more with a little extra added effort and concern. People should be happy to see each other when they come back from vacation, and clearing the deck of problems for your associates makes that happen and makes things all the better. It builds a team. The employee comes back refreshed, stays refreshed, and even refreshes the others with thankful comments about how much the easy reentry is appreciated.

3. When a company has implemented this element into policy, the vacationer knows they are not going to walk back into a fistfight on Monday morning. This adds to the effect and enjoyment of the vacation! It makes the vacation better and adds to the level of satisfaction of the employee—which is what it's all about. The effect of knowing that your teammates have your back when you are gone makes that first glass of wine on the plane sooooo much better.

4. People want bad news fast. If a problem is so tortuous that the team can't fix it, I, for one, would like to know about it before I walk into the office on my first day back. Even though I'm currently on vacation, at least that gives me a chance to create a curative plan and therefore minimize the damage. No one wants to get sucker punched on the first day back. That's when you wasted the time off.

EVERYONE in the office is your customer. That's how an engine works. Looking back over my business career, the most regretful misstep I ponder is not realizing that *all* of my fellow workers were customers. I can't recall a single situation I could have resolved or improved in instances where there was some friction between a fellow team member and myself. I didn't realize that they were not only fellow workers, they were customers as well.

Let me explain this way: Think about a car. The engine is one unit, and the carburetor is one unit, and the windshield wiper cleanser fluid is one unit, and the tires are one unit, and the windshield is a unit of the car—and so is the glove compartment, and on and on and on. So the car has a 500-horsepower engine, but the windshield wiper cleanser dispenser doesn't work. Does that detract from the quality or impression one might have of the car? Sure it does! The 500-horsepower engine looks a lot better, makes a better impression, and gets more attention if the entire car operates smoothly. Therefore, it is the business of the engine to be in a car that has no problems and runs well and performs. Otherwise, the 500-horsepower engine will be overlooked. That big strong engine will go unnoticed because a minor part of the car didn't work well.

The moral of the story: It all must work well and work well together. The same dynamic holds true for people in the business setting. Let's move the car analogy to the insurance business. Salespeople go out and call on potential clients and take them to lunch and wine and dine them and, sometimes, get to make a sale. Not an easy job. When a sale finally comes along, or a particularly difficult one to bring to fruition finally happens, the insurance policy must be reviewed by an underwriter.

On occasion, the underwriter is obliged to make the very tough decision to turn down the availability of insurance for the case or, just as troubling, drastically alter the terms. This leads to the eternal conflict between salespeople and underwriters. It is the human form of the windshield wiper cleanser getting into the grill of the 500-horsepower engines. The salesperson is now furious and is talking to the coffeepot crowd about quitting the company and moving to another insurer with more reasonable terms. But that's not going to happen—they're just blowing off steam, which doesn't do anything but poison the office.

The reality is this. The salesperson did a good job writing the policy. They did their job. So did the underwriter. It is the responsibility of the underwriter to scrub policies according to the rules and regulations of the insurer, and in doing so protect the good health of the company. If the salesperson knew the business—just a little better—they would have understood the dilemma of the underwriter and delivered the policy in a fashion with correct adjustments. The salesperson is running over to the coffeepot and telling the coffee crowd that the underwriter just cost the company a lot of money. The underwriter is telling the crew in their area that they just prevented the company from losing its backside by turning down a policy. They are talking about the very same thing, but they are not talking to each other.

Talking to each other, and communicating with each other, is what a team does and that is what teammates do—they talk to each other in an effort to improve the team. One day, the salesperson will realize that the underwriter is their "customer" and learn how to fluidly deliver a policy. Either that or they'll just keep holding court with the coffeepot crowd.

Have some pride in your organization. When we are frustrated with our job, frustrated with our place in the business world, often those emotions are easy to recognize by our co-workers, friends, and family. Just as often, we are likely to put the blame and fault of our frustration at the foot of the persons or company we work for. A common lament when one is going through this struggle is something like "This place if awful—if we only did things like..." or "I wish I had another job that took advantage of my skills," and on and on. This can be a terrible waste of time, talent, and energy. The thing to do in this instance is to dig down in your work and *lean into* the problems and frustrations you feel. Use the frustration to motivate yourself instead of letting it slow you down, making you less productive, and therefore disqualifying yourself from getting a better job. If you seek to better yourself and your career, knocking the company that is currently supplying you with a regular paycheck is not the best path to a better setting.

First of all, you owe it to your current employer, regardless of your level of frustration, to give an honest effort in return for your pay. Making a stink in your current job setting is going to do very little for you when you find your dream job and the HR department at the dream job calls your current employer for a reference. We are all guilty of this behavior, and pretty much all of us have been in this spot at one time or another in our careers.

Once I was in a job setting that was particularly exasperating to me. I wanted out. I wanted to find something else to do and other people to do it with. I came across the remarkable book titled *The Dream Manager* by Matthew Kelly. The book continually emphasized the importance of positive thinking, behaving, and visualizing. I tried like the devil to let Mr. Kelly's ideas sink into my thick head and it occurred to me, despite my self-inflicted anxiety about my current plight, that the only way out was to double down on my efforts at work and create as much of a positive aura around my division as I possibly could. It worked. One day I received a business referral, from which I received a very healthy commission check, from another division of the company that I previously had less than a stellar relationship with. Had I not rebooted my game, the referral would never have come my way.

The referral I am telling you about turned out to be an old friend I hadn't seen or talked to in years. From that reconnection came a relationship that led to a new business venture and a business partnership that exists today. Had I stayed on my self-pitying course, the referral would have never come to me. At least not from the division that sent it. Having pride in the organization and respecting the person signing my paycheck brought good fortune to me.

Want a better job and a better career? Then get better at the one you have.

Consider implementing employee contracts. I am not sure how "employee contracts" would work today, but when we used them in the late 90s and early part of Y2K they were magical. Better named "teammate contracts," here is how this worked.

Each year, I had my teammates write down their own description of their jobs. Once they completed a description of their positions, or their opinion of their tasks, I reviewed their documents and made changes I thought important. They made changes in return as well. And on and on we went until we had concluded and had a "contract" with each other regarding their responsibilities and the actions most critical to their jobs.

Sometimes the back and forth of this task became a little cumbersome and sometimes it went smooth as silk. Some contracts (all of which I still have the originals of) were half a page long and some were seven to nine pages. Some of the shorter contracts were precise and to the point, uplifting, and inspirational, as were some of the longer ones. And be assured, this was not a one-way street! I was obligated as well to write a contract describing my goals, duties, and responsibilities, of which ALL the other members of the team had the right to enjoin with codicils or recommended changes. We did this each year, around the holidays and just before the beginning of the New Year. It really made things clear to everybody about items that needed to be improved and focused on and brought everyone to an agreement about what was critical and important regarding their duties.

Not only did it bring clarity to the office setting, but it also had a more far-reaching dynamic: the suggestions made in some contracts about other members of the team—suggestions and recommendations about specific items that members of the team wanted me to emphasize with others who were falling a little short. This is what happens when you have a great team. Each team member sees to it that constant and consistent improvement is ongoing.

Another extra benefit of the contracts was the easy call to action when someone was falling short. All I had to do was sit down with the individual who was struggling, pull out our agreed-to contract, and review the agreement we had made—that we had made together.

In the early 90s, we had a team member who was a "crier." Not that it's such a bad thing to shed a tear once in a while, but this young lady cried over a pencil falling off her desk. It became quite annoying to all members of the team, and during our contract-writing phase, nearly all of the other team members asked that I emphasize with "Mary" (not her real name) that she get control of herself and stop crying every time a pressure situation popped up. So Mary and I set off on getting a mutually agreed-to contract written, and I put in the part about calling a cease to the crying … and Mary started crying. However, it turned into a revealing situation for her. She thought by crying, she would draw sympathy and calls of "poor Mary" from her buds. Now she could see that all the crying was creating were highly irritated people. Highly irritated people who didn't need to be annoyed while they were trying to do their jobs.

Mary made a great turnaround and became a critical cog in our machine. If we did not have a team atmosphere and if Mary hadn't been surrounded by stellar performers, this tack might have been an HR disaster. But in this instance it worked because everyone in the company subscribed to the same platform.

To tell the truth, most of them enjoyed the hell out of the process, and each year the contracts became more and more directed to our teammates, calling for their own self-improvement. That was a great time with great people, all of whom have gone on to successful careers. As much as anything I've engaged in managing people, the employee contract was the most synergistic, team-building exercise I have come across.

A contract is a two-way street that can turn your business into a superhighway.

Foster involvement. How many times do you hear people complain that they are not "connected" to their job? That they are not "connected" to their work? That they just want to punch the clock and get away from the people and place where they work? We can probably think of a lot of reasons why this is a constant lament. Here are a few:

- Political or philosophical divisions with the boss or the company
- Boredom with the job because it is not the kind of work they were hoping for or not the kind of work they prepared for in school
- The feeling that there is "nowhere to go" in the job—that they are "stuck"
- They don't feel "challenged" or "inspired"

There is a basic reason for all these snarls, logjams, and bottlenecks. That basic reason is this: People want to be great at their jobs. Regardless of what they might tell you, being great at their job means more to them than money or promotions or paid time off or vacation days or sick time or how much the company matches on their 401K. The desire to be great at your job is basic to human nature. Many people will challenge me on this point but I will argue it to the grave. If you are "great" at your job, all of the things above will automatically come to you—but something more important will come as well—job satisfaction. When your teammates have satisfaction in their work, they strive to be even better, and that makes the whole machine run more efficiently. The whole machine. Job satisfaction brings creativity, helpfulness to others, better working conditions, better teamwork, synergy in the workplace, and a natural way to disengage from work when away rather than worry and grind over aggravating issues.

One of the critical keys to creating this kind of involvement is the responsibility of management. Management must cast a discerning and curious eye on the level of involvement within the team. If some members of the team are unmotivated and uninspired at work, it is not hard to see or detect. That is when management has to take the extra steps to aid and motivate. Or to see if the commitment exists in the heart of the employee to take steps to become great at their job. If not, then the inevitable is obvious. But if you have a group that wants to be great, here are some ways management can help that happen:

- **Sell.** Make sure the employee knows what's in store for them if they are constantly improving at their tasks. Motivation and creativity occur when people know they are working toward a higher end.
- **Engage.** Don't be aloof—be part of the group. Let the team know you can be trusted and that you are there for them.
- **Delegate.** Stretch your employees, your team. When people find out they are trusted with responsibility they feel connected.
- **Consult.** Don't lose contact with your team. Stay connected to them. Encourage participation in team meetings and have regular individual meetings. When people can express themselves, great things happen and bad stuff does not build up.

The more you involve your team, the more efficient ALL the pieces will be. A 500-horsepower engine won't work well with a bad sparkplug.

Empowerment—the best way to safeguard expenses and raise revenue. In this section, the internal customer service section, we have talked about a lot of issues, including:

- Why internal customer service is the second step to building a great organization
- The fact that everyone in your organization is your customer—not just another co-worker
- The importance of pride in your organization
- The effective use of contracts with your team and why "spelling it out" with your co-workers and teammates is so effective
- The importance of involvement

All these issues move the team and the individual team members toward empowerment. When members of the team feel empowered, great dividends begin to happen. And when people have pride in what they do because of feeling empowered and important, some remarkable things begin to happen. People take ownership of issues and see to it they're handled correctly. This comes from the pride and importance they feel about their company and co-workers and the resultant determination to see to it that things are done right.

Here is an example. When I operated my own mortgage company, Paul Karem Mortgage, I trained my team to do things that mortgage processors did not regularly do at other mortgage companies. One of those duties was allowing the mortgage processors to "lock" loans that were in process. Locking a loan, in mortgage parlance, means creating the contract on the interest rate for a predetermined period of time. In other words, when someone has applied for a mortgage loan, they are then locked, if they so choose, to the prevailing rate at the time for either 15, 45, or 60 days—or until the loan closes. Some people choose to "float" the rate in hopes that the rates fall, which can sometimes be a disastrous choice. Nonetheless, I afforded my processors the authority to lock loans after they showed the desire and acumen to handle the responsibility.

Not once did I have a problem with a locked loan. The team performed the duty with precise accuracy. Why? Because they understood the critical importance of protecting the interest rates, for the company and the borrower, and accepted the responsibility of the duty. Not only was the duty of great importance to the processors, it also created other efficiencies within the team. Those included:

- Our company never had any issues with honoring interest rate commitments, nor did we ever have a loan go exposed because a lock was overlooked. Either of these situations can spell financial doom for a mortgage company.

- My time was freed up for selling and marketing, which brought more production into the organization.

- The support team took their lock authority seriously—with the appropriate amount of caution—which empowered them and showed them how important they were to the organization.

- 100% of our loans closed without any controversy about rates or fees because of the way the processors communicated with the borrowers.

- The processors scoured all 21 of our lenders (the entities that we delivered our loans to) to find the very best rates for the borrowers. Again, another timesaver for the salespeople.

When people feel empowered, they will watch revenues and expenses like they would watch their own. Of course, these kinds of responsibilities can happen only with the proper amount of training—which is yet another way to build trust and internal customer service. Never put a teammate in harm's way on the job by launching them into a task before they are properly prepared. Once prepared, it is human nature to do the job well. Empowerment—the best way to create exemplary internal customer service.

Review

If you do not have internal customer service, the external customer is not going to have an interest in doing business with you. If you do not have internal customer service, the external customer is going to know it immediately. When you enter a restaurant and the hostess, chef, waiter, and bartender are not on the same page, or in sync with each other, you know it before you get your salad. This is true of any business or industry. The lack of internal customer service will shove the external customer out the door. Each of the pieces touched on in this section add or detract to the level of internal customer service in your organization. Those pieces include:

- Having individuals who manage themselves in a professional manner for the good of the whole
- Combining self-managing individuals, molding self-managing individuals, into a team
- Having clarity on the issue of each of your co-workers being your customer. And each of those co-workers understanding that you are their customer as well. Having an understanding of this can be exactly what is needed to create a great company and form a great individual career. Everyone in the organization has to understand how to work as a team. Along with that comes the understanding that all of the team members are critical to your individual success. Even the world's best opera singer must understand and function as part of a team. If the world's best opera singer has no

orchestra, no sheet music, and no stage hands to set the scenes, their talent is for naught. The same is true of the dynamic sales-person who battles with the CFO or the underwriter or the stalwart bricklayer who can't get along with the foreman. In all instances, these conflicts are detrimental to the success of the entire team and the individuals as well.

- If you don't have pride in your company, do everyone who works with you a favor and get another job. Why? Because they already know you feel this way, and that alone is dragging down the spir-it of your co-workers. We have all been in frustrating situations where we held court as the solvers of all the company problems BUT that same amount of energy is better served finding solutions and building esprit de corps. It is much easier to solve problems than to discuss them over and over and over.

- If you have run out of ideas about how to create great synergy in your organization, try individual contracts with your associates. This gives everyone a chance to say what's on their mind and put in writing exactly what is expected of each other. More important-ly, you can come away with an agreement on lingering issues, put them to bed, and use the same energy doing something productive.

- If you are not involved in the processes and undertakings of your organization, then get involved. Go to your associates and manag-ers and find a way to use your individual talents to a higher good.

- If you are not empowering others, delegating to your team, you are not as good a manager as you could be. Two heads are better than one, so wouldn't it follow that the same would hold true for 10, 20, 30, or more heads?

Illustration by Steve Ford down at the Tollhouse

"These damn customers!! How annoying!!"

Chapter Six: The benefits of customer service excellence

Clarity. Achieving great customer service, internal and external, in your organization can bring a number of rewarding and lasting benefits. One of the foremost of those benefits is clarity regarding your job and your role. This goes a little further than one thinks because great customer service will bring an individual to a point where they realize what business they are truly in. For example, being in the mortgage business gives one many ways to approach marketing the business. You can concentrate on offering refinance options, you can do all your marketing over the internet, and you can call on money managers or other financial professionals to try to build your line of business by securing referrals.

For Paul Karem Mortgage, our main concentration of business marketing was directed at realtors—realtors who sell homes and give some counsel or advice to the homebuyer about which sources their customers might consider for their mortgage financing. We developed the trust of realtors who were confident that referring customers to us would result in well-handled, hands-on financing.

With that said, there comes a clarity about what business we are were REALLY in. We were in the "realtor customer service" business. My company did not write the underwriting requirements for mortgage lending or determine the path of interest rates. That is/was done by Fannie Mae and Freddie Mac and all the other places where mortgages are eventually delivered. Our mission was to get the mortgage from application to closing in the most secure, professional, hands-on manner. That is done in a fashion to gain the trust and confidence of the borrowers, whom we are obligated to, and the realtors who referred the loan to us.

Getting the trust of realtors today is not an easy job. The advent of mortgages originated on the internet and in-house lending within the realtor's offices has made securing realtor clients all the more difficult. So it stands to reason that getting realtors as trusted sources of referral today requires exceptional performance. The best way to distinguish yourself in the market, given the tough competition that exists, falls to customer service excellence.

A close friend of mine owns a trucking company. He often tells his employees the following: "We are not in the trucking business ... we are in the business of making money." Another close associate is in the heating and cooling business. His advisement to his team is this: "We are not in the heating and cooling business; we are in the response business."

Become great at your job

Young people tell me all the time, "I want to make more money." Well, the best way to make more money is to become great at your job. If you are great at your job, the issue of making money will be five or six steps down the line in importance because greatness in your work will bring the money to your doorstep. Companies seek out those who are exceptional in their work because there are damn few people in that category. Therefore, those who excel in their jobs will be able to draw and negotiate peak salaries because the market is going to seek them out.

And the best way to be great at your job, the best way to excel at your job, the best way to perform at a level of excellence in your job, is when you embrace and understand internal and external customer service. When you are great at customer service, you separate yourself from the competition because that skill alone will make you unique in the marketplace. Remember the premise of this book—America's Customer Service Disaster—which is the element in today's business world that will make your service excellence stand out.

Terrible customer service is omnipresent in business today. To prove my point (if it needs proof), all you have to do is look at successful companies and all the successful careers they create. The examples are endless. And they all have a common denominator—great customer service! Want more money? Then get it the smartest and best way: Embrace and practice great customer service. Understand that everyone you work with, in one way or another, is your customer, and you are theirs. Understand that an issue with a disgruntled customer is not a personal slap in your face. It is an opportunity to fix the issue and turn the disgruntled customer into an advocate.

When you are around greatness, you learn how to be great. Let's use football for example. Paul W. "Bear" Bryant is regarded in some circles as the greatest college football coach in history. Being around the greatness of Coach Bryant showed a lot of young men how to be great football players, and a LOT more. Not only did many of his players become professional football players, but as many or more of his players became doctors and lawyers. One staggering statistic about Coach Bryant is the number of his assistant coaches who became head coaches at other major colleges or head coaches in the National Football League. Forty of Bryant's assistants became head coaches. His former assistants won conference and national championships and too many games to count. There was a reason. When you are around greatness you learn what it looks and feels like. Then you have a blueprint if you are interested in becoming great yourself. In the business world, customer service excellence is the best way to become great at your work.

Build a REAL team

Definition of team: A number of persons associated together in work or activity. (*Webster's*)

As simple as that definition sounds, few people in the business world get to know what being part of a team is really like. I have had the fortune of being part of a team three times in my business career. I have had the misfortune of being in groups that were lightyears away from being a team as well. Even though those groups were "associated together in work," as the definition above states, those associated were not blended together in spirit.

Before a real team can be formed, the entire group has to be on the same page. As we stated before, there are three steps to forming a great team:

1. You must have individuals who self-manage, with drive and ambition, for the good of the whole.
2. Those self-managing parts must form into a cohesive team with the same mission, goals, principles, and intentions. AND those self-managing parts must engage each other as customers. If numbers 1 and 2 happen, then comes number 3.
3. The external customers will knock the door down to do business with you.

If some of the individual parts are not on the same page, the team experience will not happen. Consider the sporting world. Some professional teams, with individual parts that make millions and millions of dollars, are perennial losers. Year after year after year after year. On the other hand, some professional teams win championships consistently. The talent levels between these winning and losing teams is not the element that makes the big difference. Professional sports franchises not only spend millions on player contracts, they spend millions appraising and evaluating talent. All athletes who make a living playing a sport are the best of the best of the best of the best.

So why the big difference in their winning and losing records? Some are blended into a team and some are a bunch of individuals. That's the answer. The same holds true in business. Some businesses have individuals who work till 9:00 at night with smiles on their faces and some have individuals who hit the door at 5:00 o'clock on the dot, regardless of what kind of mess is left behind. And that mess is left for others to clean up.

When you have a group of talented people, together in business, who understand internal and external customer service, you have the rare opportunity for magic in the marketplace. But if a business venture gets off on the wrong foot with disconnected people, consider the following from *Fox Business* in a May 2017 article: "Roughly 20% of new businesses survive past their first year of operation. That was the case two decades ago and is still the case today."

Yikes. That's pretty scary. It is also glaring proof that the way to sustain business and separate from the competition is customer service excellence. The businesses that are failing are not people trying to sell 13-inch rulers. They are real businesses in industries that thrive and succeed. They are restaurants, retail stores, coffee houses, brokerage houses, and the like. The difference between succeeding and failing in business is that success requires all the parts to be pulling in the same direction, for the same purpose.

When internal customer service exists in the workplace, the rewarding experience of real team synergy occurs. This can be one of the most gratifying rewards in business. The team environment is the catalyst for the most enriching, uplifting condition in the business setting, *blurring the lines* between work, home, and vacation. When you are part of a real team, you don't return from vacation worrying about the mess awaiting you. Why? Because there will not be one. When you are part of a real team, you engage with your associates in a way that makes your performance, their performance, and the performance of the whole team more effective and productive. When you are part of a real team, your mind is not cluttered with worry when you get home at 6:00 o'clock. When you are part of a real team, a vacation becomes rewarding and uplifting because you recover your mojo as opposed to worrying about how things are going to be handled while you are gone.

I wish I could give you better examples than those, but I guess this might be the best way to explain: Once you have been part of a real team, should you ever join another company where the team is disconnected, it is grueling to endure. Once you have been in a situation where your team was the best, it is tough as hell to be part of a team that is a big pile of individuals and not a real team. Just as tough to survive is the attitude of the individual who really has no idea of what it's like to blend into a team because it will be next to impossible for you to explain to that person what team really means. When you are part of the disconnected group, rest assured you will be miserable when you return from vacation.

Great customer service helps you recruit top talent that wants to win and wants to work with you

People want to be on a winning team. People want to be around successful people and successful businesses. When you go shopping, you don't search for the store with the worst inventory and the worst service. You search for the store with the best quality and prices and friendly customer service. It then follows that when you are searching for a job or a better workplace to further your career, you are going to seek out successful businesses that provide value and customer service. You are going to be drawn to being part of a winning team. That's one reason why professional athletes sometimes seek to be traded to teams with good chances of winning championships. Regardless of the huge money some professional athletes make, they are still drawn to their ultimate goal—being part of a championship team.

By the same token, if you are already on the championship team, others are going to want to join your group. Building your team, your business, by providing customer service excellence, internal and external, will draw talent to you, 365/24/7. And attracting candidates for hire by having them seek you out pays a lot of dividends. Some of those are

- People who have sought you out come to work with a different attitude than most. They are ready and open to learning how to be part of a successful team, and that means they are ready to listen, be managed, and molded into a piece of the team.

- These new folks do not come in with an attitude that they are going to swing their weight around and show their new comrades how to do things. To the contrary, they are primed for listening and learning—not preaching or rocking the boat.

- You don't have to spend money recruiting and paying personnel firms. Your standing in the marketplace, which is a byproduct of customer service excellence, is your personnel recruiting agency.

- The person who seeks employment with a firm noted for customer service is equipped with the level of empathy that fits into the organization. They are coming to you because your company's performance has struck a nerve with them. Maybe because they are not able to perform to the level they desire in their current job. Or maybe they are the type who are driven to provide good customer skills but can't do so in their current position because of a differing, less customer-friendly approach by current management and the surroundings. Believe me, a lot of people in that category are out there looking for a company that assists in providing service excellence. And they want to be as much a part of that as the elite athlete wants to win championships. There is a large pool of job applicants in this category, which makes your selection process deep and wide—much wider than an employment agency can provide.

- Sometimes, and I have experienced this more than once, someone seeking to join your team will come with a written plan of what they are going to do for your company and how they are going to do it. Once I even had a candidate make a sale during the interview. This particular gentleman, upon overhearing an associate of mine telling me there was trouble moving a product, said, "Mr. Karem, I can sell some of those for you." Then he took the phone and did just that. Yes, I hired him.

When you provide trendsetting customer service, you have created your own personnel recruiting agency. The applicants are watching your performance from a large, large audience. And the best of the best will come to you. Some of the best partners and teammates I have ever worked with came to my companies seeking out a position because they heard of the level of job satisfaction and the level of customer satisfaction we provided.

Great customer service creates the world's best advertising agency

There are many ways to advertise, but my guess is that we can all agree on which way might be the very best: WORD OF MOUTH. Maybe today, word of mouth could even be labeled "click of mouse," since a disgruntled customer can easily tell the story of their woe to all their email contacts with a single click.

When you have won over your client base with better-than-expected service levels, your client base will become part of your sales and marketing team. They will go out of their way to tell family, friends, and business associates how well they were treated—especially now, with the miserable level of customer service that exists in all lines of business.

Word of mouth is more respected and trusted than TV advertising (especially today!), putting your company name on a billboard, or blasting out self-praise over the radio airwaves. Countless businesses have built and sustained success with little, if any, expenditures on advertising. However, the one thing those companies have in common is the vibrant respect they have created with their customer base and the vibrant way those customers tell the story of their service experience.

Word of mouth has helped me travel a long way in the mortgage industry, and here's an example. Today, many mortgage companies rely heavily on home refinancing to build and sustain their business. Granted, in some cases refinancing your home mortgage can help pay down high interest debt, remove credit card debt, pay for college tuition, and take some financial pressure off. But a lot of the reasons companies use to encourage people to refinance are not in the best interest of the borrower—they are in the best interest of the mortgage company that is writing the business.

Some companies would have their mortgage holders refinance over and over and over again, which essentially amounts to "churning" the customer. When you give people the best advice and counsel, you get dividends for holding true to the interest of the customer. And sometimes those dividends come from sources you never could have imagined. Often I advise my clients NOT to refinance their homes. Why? Because it's not always in the customers' best interest.

Let me explain. Once, a former borrower came to me and wanted to refinance his loan because the available interest rate was 3% lower than his current rate and the payment would lower by more than $800.00 per month. After looking at the scenario, I advised him not to refinance and to leave his mortgage as it was. Why? Because he was in the 11th year of his current loan and he was beginning to pay more principle than interest on his loan every month. Had he refinanced his loan at the lower rate, he would have given up the accelerating principle payments and gone back to the start of a 30-year amortization, with the preponderance of his payments going to interest! I advised not to refinance and he was grateful for the direction. This led to the word-of -mouth benefit, as he told a number of associates about his experience, and a good deal of them ended up doing business with my company.

A simple formula when you think about people: Give them the truth and the best advice, and they will give you good word-of-mouth. Another way to create word-of-mouth goodwill is to treat everybody with the same level of care and respect. You never know who you are talking to. Just because someone is not dressed to the nines does not mean they are not influential and a strong referral source. You may be speaking to a C-suite executive who manages hundreds of people, is a dynamic leader, and has strong influence over them. Regardless of whom you are addressing, make sure you give them your very best and they will represent you well with the story they tell of your regard for them!

Great customer service eliminates "poison" on the team

If you develop great customer service in your organization, it raises sensitivity and awareness within the team. It creates awareness about internal and external customer service and about the way team members carry themselves with their associates. Great teams will create a poor stage for naysayers and those who are inclined to knock everything—including the boss, the product, the external customers, and most harmful of all, the other associates.

Poison within the team is a business cancer. A college football player was recently interviewed on *Sports Center* after a huge victory. What was especially exciting about the big win was that it was accomplished by a school whose football history has been less than stellar. To put it bluntly, this particular school has been at the bottom of the barrel for a long, long time. So when asked about how his team was able to pull off the amazing upset, the player responded, "We don't have any guys whispering in corners anymore." *Whispering in corners.* Does that strike a chord with you? Have you been around those types, the corner whisperers? They can destroy a team or a business organization in short order.

Politics today and the separation in our society as a result of the combative political environment have created the perfect storm for negative behavior and negative, undermining self-conduct. Every political contest or election, be it state, county, local, or federal, is packed with the worst kind of vitriol and negative dialogue. We are marinated in it. So it stands to reason that some would pick up the style and manner of all this confrontational, accusatory behavior and try to perfect it. After all, it is the political order of the day. And if our leaders are behaving this way, and in doing so getting elected to high office, why not use the same tactics in business to get a promotion or win a battle with a co-worker? A bad situation to say the least.

But let's dial back to the first sentence in this section: If you develop great customer service in your organization, it raises sensitivity and awareness within the team. If you have great customer service in your team, in your organization, the poison, the whisperers in the corner, will not survive. Why? Because within a team or organization built on customer service, those kinds of behavior and tactics will be rejected and made to look foolish. The purveyors of such antics will quickly see that their methods are ineffective and unpopular and they will take a hike or will be hitchhiked out of the office. Or maybe, just maybe, they will get it and have a brain-opening experience that enables them to latch onto the bright side of their talents and use them in a positive way.

If the team is already flawed with poison, the positive energy will be drained right out of the productive performer and their choice will be simple—

join the club or move on to a different company. Just consider how many productive, positive people, and customers, have been lost to companies where "poisoning the team" dialogue wins the day.

Create great customer service in your organization and it will pay a lot of dividends. One of the most beneficial and rewarding might be the large exit sign for poison!

Great customer service creates leaders

In much the same way that internal customer service eliminates poison in an organization, it also creates leaders who safeguard the mission and direction of the organization. According to *Webster's*, a leader, by definition, is a person who has commanding authority or influence. "Commanding authority or influence" is a great thing to be around, but leaders created by virtue of great internal customer service are not always "authorities." As a matter of fact, most great leadership in standout companies comes from the general population of dedicated employees—employees who are dedicated to the success of the company they work for and dedicated as well to seeing that their associates do not hinder that success by customer service failings.

Leaders take care of the business and the people in the business in a way that causes a kind of centrifugal force, where the benefit and effect of their leadership is increased by example and the creation of more leaders. This dynamic can work both ways. As illustrated by "The Ringleader, the Follower, and the Protégé," discussed in the chapter on thin-skinned behavior, some leaders have their own ideas and methods about how things should go. And some of those are motivated by self-interest and the urge to get ahead of others.

We have all experienced these types in business. Mostly they rule by force or intimidation and can get away with administering their agenda because of the lack of people around them who are ready and willing to challenge their behavior. When you have great internal customer service, these types can't prevail and either choose to join the team or join another team where they might be able to secure the bully pulpit. Once you are relieved of the presence of those who peddle negative behavior, you have a real chance to move close to "blurring the lines."

The benefits of creating leaders in your organization are many, including:

People reach into their self-realization and confidence.

When real leaders are present, they look after the good of the individual as well as the whole. One important mission of an effective leader is seeing to it that members of the team develop personal skills and overcome barriers that are holding them back. When I was young and in school, my summer job was in a meat processing company owned by one of my uncles. I was mesmerized by the skill of the butchers and meat cutters. I was dazzled watching these men break down hindquarters and forequarters of beef so efficiently, so fast, and so perfectly. One day my uncle handed me a boning knife and said "Here, break down this forequarter." Scared the hell out of me. But … he stood there and watched me stumble through the process, correcting me along the way. When we were done I felt 10 feet tall and ready to break down all the sides in the locker. That's what leaders do.

People who are led by "real leaders" are not afraid to make mistakes.

With the kind of leadership described above, people become less hesitant to push themselves a little more than usual and are not so worried about messing something up. This comes from knowing that the presence of a leader will offer assurances that whatever the problem, it will be taken care of. Like the old saying, "You can't get to second base unless you take your foot off first." Sometimes it is hard to engage a real challenge to do something you are a little afraid of doing. But the reality of business is that it is rare to find a lasting career by doing the same things at the same skill levels over time. Being around positive leaders makes work exciting, energizing, and challenging in a creative way. Great leaders are not as worried about mistakes as they are hopeful that people on their team are willing to stretch themselves. Remember, rough seas make better sailors!

Great leadership, from top to bottom, improves listening and communication skills

There's a wonderful old saying, "God gave us one mouth and two ears. One of them closes; the other two don't." When there is trust in the leadership of a company, and that same leadership creates additional leaders, communication becomes effective in a way that is rare in business today. First of all, team members come to trust their leaders and co-workers, which eliminates poison in the workplace and makes everyone more productive. Secondly, suggestions or advisements or constructive criticism that might be taken the wrong way in a setting with poor leadership are not met with paper-thin sensitivities and resistance. Possibly more than eliminating fear of mistakes and bolstering self-confidence, the creation of new leaders in an organization improves morale and efficiency!

Great customer service distinguishes you in the marketplace.

How many times have you been pleased and surprised when you called a business and the phone was answered by a human being in courteous helpful fashion? Did you decide right then to do business with that company, and those people again? How many times have you been surprised and delighted when you had a problem with a company you were doing business with, and it corrected the problem? Probably not very often. How many times have you decided to forego doing business with a company that fell short in its customer service commitment, causing you to find another provider? Probably pretty often.

How many times have you experienced an incorrect billing or invoice for goods or services—and tried to get the invoice corrected—and found that your efforts to fix the problem were almost more taxing than the frustration of being overcharged? That happens often today. People and companies sometimes alter agreements midstream to make an additional buck or two. Happens a lot in my industry, mortgage lending.

How many times have you had a problem with a company and were required to explain the situation in its entirety to more than one person, over and over and over? I am talking about the instance where you give the first customer service rep your name, social security number, verifying cell or office number, and the account number, and then have to repeat all that to another person 10 minutes later. All of these examples have become commonplace. And what a *great opportunity* that is for you and your business.

Great customer service, internal and external, distinguishes you in the marketplace today like never before. The simple act of courteous, thoughtful customer service can increase your market share, earnings, and reputation in your industry and pack your wallet like nothing else. No online business course or seminar can come close to what providing great customer service will do for your career. The customer service environment of today is so lacking that even basic cordiality and manners can separate you from your competition. There's never been an opportunity like this. And the opportunity does not limit itself to behavior. A better use of technology, formed from the commentary of your customer base, can jettison your business or career. And don't forget the 3rd piece of America's Customer Service Disaster—the Disconnect. A good alternative to self-praise in media advertising is an honest dialogue with the viewer/listener. Just tell them the truth in your appeal to the customer. Consumer ears are starving for the truth.

So there you have the multiple benefits of great customer service:

- Clarity about what your mission REALLY is
- A chance to be GREAT at your job
- A chance to create a TEAM
- The best way to RECRUIT
- World's best advertising—WORD OF MOUTH
- A way to eliminate POISION on the team
- The opportunity to create LEADERS
- A chance to DISTINGUISH yourself in the marketplace

What seminar or webinar or online course or self-help coach can do THAT!?

Chapter Seven: The future of customer service

We are in the throes of America's Customer Service Disaster. We are surrounded by the current level of service in all three phases of ACSD. Where do consumers go from here? Are we compelled to succumb to insolent behavior and the maddening way technology is misused? Will the next generation of those seeking their first job come into the marketplace completely void of customer skills and unaware that there is any need for those skills?

It looks bleak but WAIT! Help is on the way! There is a forthcoming mandate from consumers demanding customer service from every corner of business. CS reps, physicians, razor blade companies, taxi companies, fast food stores, retail stores, airlines, mortgage companies, even public servants are all entering into a time when the demand for service excellence will take on a nearly combative insistence from consumers. Consumers now have more ways to express satisfaction with goods and service providers than ever before. The story of a bad customer experience can be launched into the sphere of general knowledge using chat rooms, Facebook, customer service reviews, letters to the editor, Twitter, Glassdoor, consumer reports, texting, word of many mouths, TestFreaks, and many more, all the way up to our old buddy J.D. Power. Today, it is virtually impossible to hide lousy customer service—especially by using self-praising media ads. The consumer can't be fooled anymore and that reality has to sink into the mindset of elite and rank-and-file workers. Consider some of the calls to action suggested by various articles.

Field Service News describes the skills technicians will need in the immediate future. Those include:

- More responsive, courteous, on-time performance in the field. This is a call to action for the cable installers, HVAC technicians, electricians, and plumbers who are a little tardy and not up on their tippy toes when they are face to face with the customer.

- *Field Service News* also outlines the certain need for proactive salesmanship and social skills required if the technician of today/ tomorrow wants to have a long and rewarding career.
- Mastery of mobile technology, in the same manner that Uber has used so effectively, is a skill that will become commonplace rather than exceptional if the tech wants to survive.

Zendesk calls for the following from techs:

- MIRROR the customer's manner and tone.
- LISTEN first—then validate the problem.
- SUMMARIZE your help.
- MAKE templates your own—don't be a robot.
- Be COMFORTABLE with multitasking—it means you are BUSY, which is good.
- RESPOND on social media when necessary.

These are issues the technician of yesterday did not consider, with the exception of those who are naturally gifted with helpful instincts. Here is the good news: The multiple calls to action listed above are not admonishments or caustic reviews of techies and geeks. They are the roadmap to the bank!

The opportunity to distinguish yourself in a sea of same

Much of corporate America looks and acts in the same manner, failing badly in trying to achieve an effective mandate on customer service. Everybody is doing things the same way. All have jumped on the same treadmill—and it's not taking them where they want to go. Not only do they use voice mail ineffectively, they are now mirroring one another with the same strategies that frustrate the hell out of the external customers.

In lockstep, corporate America is now asking the consumer to use portals to open simple emails, requiring passwords and IDs for the most fundamental information exchange, and has latched onto the new fashion in texting—"I can't talk right now"—along with all the other latest fads. All seem to jump aboard and accept this same way of doing things, and, in doing so, end up providing the customer with the same frustrations and the same dissatisfaction. It is as if they have collectively strategized methods that keep the external customer at bay. Or ... AWAY.

As stated over and over in this book, what this boils down to is a terrific opportunity. The current assembly line stratagems discussed here bring about an easy and obtainable opportunity to distinguish yourself from the crowd and from the competition. Look at your communications to the external customer through their eyes, not the eyes of internal procedure. While all your competitors are copying each other with the latest ways to keep the customer at a distance, you can extend a hand and invite the customer in. The difference in customer service today between the dedicated provider and those left wanting has never been wider or more distinct. And that difference will result in a very distinct difference in checkbook balances!

Few businesses have a more convoluted gauntlet for the customer to travel than the residential mortgage business. Because of the mortgage mess of 2008, the U.S. government changed, altered, and substantially rewrote mortgage laws and regulations. Changes came full tilt in an effort to avoid the same troubles that surfaced with the highly risky subprime lending and credit swaps that some large institutions gobbled up. Certainly these changes were well-intended, but they brought volumes of forms and disclosures that are confusing, at best, to the consumer. One day, sooner rather than later, a lender is going to learn how to navigate these mandates in a more efficient and customer-friendly manner than the industry now handles all this. Just as Uber found a way to challenge taxis by applying customer-friendly technology and an inexpensive price point, the same thing can happen in a lot of industries. It has even happened in the men's razor business—a business that has held to the same business models for a hundred years! The opportunity exists today for a company, or even an entire industry, to gain prominence simply by embracing the customer and giving them the path of least resistance.

Don't jump in the sea of same. Think of a better mousetrap!

If there is a way to knock your business, social media WILL find it ☹

When something goes wrong for one of your customers, you can be sure that the chance exists that one helluva of lot of people are going to hear about it. Today, the frustrated customer has found no relief by going back to the business where they were ill-treated or badly served in the first place. The frustrated customer gains no solace in trying to resolve the issue they have endured by reaching out to the same entity that authored the issue. Just as companies and businesses have digressed in providing customer service, they are equally inept at solving the problems and complaints caused by the same bad customer service.

Recently my wife experienced terrible, and somewhat embarrassing, customer treatment at a new hotel here in Louisville. The story of the incident is not important—just know that the aftermath, and the efforts made to pull a simple apology out of these people, were as frustrating as the initial experience. I called the hotel four times in an effort to describe the issue. Four times. Each time I called, I asked for someone in management. Each time I called and made the request to speak to management it was handled with adept skill at moving the call down the line or asking if management could call me back—which never happened. Clearly these well-behaved and well-intended call handlers had more training on how to guard management from disgruntled customers than management had in providing service to customers. They almost sounded embarrassed when trying to move my call away from "management"—proof that the basic instinct one has still tilts toward helpful and courteous assistance.

Curious to note that this hotel, a remarkable and physically astounding structure, still functioned in this instance as poorly, or worse, than some of the previously noted providers of awful service. The Omni Hotel paid 52 percent of the development costs ($150 million), and the city and state provided 48 percent ($139 million) of the 289 million bucks it took to raise this hotel. The Omni hotel even has a $17 million garage! One would think with all that money and support from our city and state that some of the money could be spent on learning how to treat a customer. Maybe they could have reduced the garage budget to $16,999,000 and spent the remaining dollars on phone training for "management."

The point of all this is that if you provide poor customer service, people are sure to hear about it. The fact remains that people love to relay bad news, now more than ever. And if the issue is not resolved, all you are doing is motivating the aggravated customer to tell the story on Facebook or LinkedIn or Twitter or Instagram or any of the other dozens of ways to get the story in front of thousands of people or more. Or maybe even write about it in a book.

The initial customer service offense is troubling enough.

When the customer is not given satisfaction, or even the opportunity to state their case, the offense becomes AIRBORNE!

Who will occupy the C-suites?

Has this trend run its course? Is the Age of Rude coming to an end? I believe it is. I believe the evidence of the benefits of exceptional customer service are too strong for the bad service trends and habits to continue. The overwhelming success of the refined customer service providers is showing up in reputation, bulging checkbooks, and rising stock prices. This is all being witnessed by the next generation of leadership, and the next generation of leadership is not interested in mediocrity. The next generation of C-suite executives, having witnessed the downfall of crappy, frustrating service platforms, will better understand the need for service excellence, having endured it themselves both as middle managers and as consumers.

The next generation of C-suite executives will study some of the remarkable turnarounds that large companies have accomplished by revamping their entire customer service platforms—not by constructing new buildings or trying to cajole consumers with laudatory media ads. They will have seen the great turnarounds of Delta, General Motors, and even Old Spice, all in no small part due to a greater understanding of customer service. Consider the following facts published in the onereach.com blog:

- It is six to seven times more expensive to attract a new customer than to keep an existing one. (Office of Consumer Affairs).
- A large increase in customer retention can result in a 30 percent increase in company value. (Bain & Co.)
- More than 65 percent of consumers say that valuing their time is the most important thing a company can do to provide good online service. (NICE)
- More than 60 percent of companies think mobile customer service is a competitive differentiator. (CMI)
- 74 percent have spent MORE in response to great customer service. (American Express)
- U.S. companies (currently the home court of bad customer service) lose approximately $41 billion annually due to bad customer

service. (SmartCustomerService)

- A 5 percent increase in customer retention can increase profits by up to 125 percent. (Bain & Co)

You can bet your gizzard that the new occupiers of C-suites will know, study, and embrace these kinds of statistics and facts. And the other distinguishing characteristic of the new C-suite exec is that they will pour the knowledge of the stats above into the one place that can make all the magic happen: internal customer service.

Don't say we didn't warn you

Have you seen the pharmaceutical commercials on TV with the *endless* disclosures? Is that going to become commonplace for ALL industries?

You know the medical commercials on TV, and in other print and media ads, that I am referring to. They all pretty much follow the same pattern—a portion of the piece talks about the benefits of the product and then at least half of the ad is devoted to every single thing that can go wrong if you take the advertised drug or medicine. I assume this is all done under the direction of legal protection. I guess the companies are relieved of any legal obligation, having declared the possibility that the medicine or drug can cause bad side effects.

According to an article in *Policy and Medicine*, the United States Food and Drug Administration (FDA) initiated plans in September 2018 to study the usefulness, if any, of these disclosures in prescription and drug advertisements. So after all the millions of dollars spent on the ads and the actors in the ads and the scripts, Big Brother is taking a look to see if the ads make any difference at all.

I wonder if this manner of advertising will leak out to other lines of business and industries. I wonder if the stating of things that can go wrong, thus relieving the wrongdoer of liability, will take flight in the promotion of products outside the prescription and drug industry. The providers of poor service would probably be the first to jump on this bandwagon. Maybe we are at a critical point where customer service becomes secondary to protective measures that cover the service providers' booty. Will we soon be listening to long, drawn-out disclosures during media ads for a lengthy list of products beyond drugs and prescriptions? I certainly hope not.

Should this become a trend, it will most certainly provide a large opportunity for businesses that understand customer service. Trying to explain away a service shortfall to a consumer by listing all the reasons the responsibility lies elsewhere—even if legitimate—is the last thing the consumer wants to hear. Not only is it the last thing they want to hear, it also takes more time and energy from the service provider than simply fixing the problem. You have probably worked with a person like this before. They will take more time dodging the issue than the easy path to a solution would require.

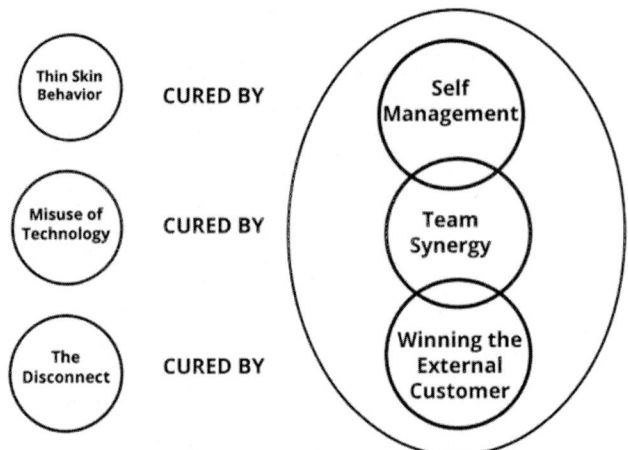

Achieving the 3 components of customer service excellence
Creates
Teamwork, innovation, creativity in workplace, customer attraction, financial success, professional success

BLURS THE LINES BETWEEN WORK, HOME & VACATION

Review

The future of customer service is at hand. It includes:

Bad news for techs

Get off the treadmill!

Be aware of social media—it is sure as hell aware of YOU.

Your next CEO or CFO or COO. Better brush up on your service skills to prepare to work with them.

Fix the problem. No one wants to hear a history lesson.

Chapter Eight: The opportunity

Customers are BEGGING for an honest dialogue.

As stated many times prior in this book—you cannot fool the customer anymore. The internet and easy-to-reach information have made the consumer more demanding, price-conscious, and savvy. All of which adds up to a bad situation for a company or business with poor service habits and poor service personnel. That's the bad news. Here is the good news: Like never before, it is easy to distinguish yourself or your business by doing the simple things that send out an inviting message to your customer.

All the success you can imagine is out their waiting for you. All it requires is a sensitivity to the customer and the customer's issues. America's Customer Service Disaster has put you in position to achieve the success you've dreamed of—and it has never been easier to gain an advantage with great customer service!

I started my own mortgage company, Paul Karem Mortgage, in 2000. I sold the company to a regional bank in 2006, a decision I regret to this day. The bank was a wonderful, solid partner with a winning reputation, but my regret stemmed from letting go of a unique brand of customer service that I had built. The cornerstone of my company was the catch phrase "No Voice Mail During Office Hours."

When I coined that phrase, I was told by a very successful realtor, whom I had targeted as a customer, "That's a cute saying Paul, but it will never work." Well, turns out it worked in a big way. In 2002, with a staff of five people, my firm closed more dollar volume and units than a competitor with a staff of 116. Was I that much more talented or smarter than my competition? Hell no. To the contrary, I am sure they were more gifted intellectually than me. But I understood what the customer wanted and how the customer wanted to be treated. All the talent and intellect in the world becomes ineffective if you can't deliver your product to a willing customer base.

They are not only waiting—THEY ARE BEGGING.

Customers are begging for courtesy

We are divided socially and politically today in a big way. Maybe as much or more than ever before. People make assumptions about those they meet in microseconds and form their reactions and behaviors around those assumptions. What happened to "courtesy" in our society? Where in the world did it go? And how did it leave us so fast? Maybe the current trend of the body politic took it away from us. Maybe the annoying, unceasing acrimony between political enemies pulled us into the state of absent courtesy. Maybe AM radio took it away by hosting sports talk shows, and political talk shows, with people screaming at one another, unable to hear each other because they're all talking and screaming at the same time.

Common courtesy is gone. Not only is it hard to find in everyday society, it is uncommonly rare in business as well. The absence of common courtesy brings you the opportunity of a natural way to distinguish yourself in the business setting. It brings you the opportunity to set yourself apart from the competition simply by embracing a natural human instinct—*the natural spirit of helpfulness.* Is there anything more rewarding than being helpful to another person? I am sure there have been times in your life when someone recounted some way you served them that helped them through a difficult time or issue. And I am sure that hearing the praise of your service was very rewarding.

The dividend that helpfulness pays is available to all of us. Think about that for a second. The dividend that helpfulness pays is available to all of us. Unlike a certificate of deposit, you don't have to wait a long time to collect the dividends payable from serving someone with common courtesy. They are available immediately. And today, like never before, common courtesy stands out in uncommon fashion.

The current marinade of vindictive dialogue that we are all soaking in has make simple, natural, and easy- to-master courtesy techniques stand out like never before. And those techniques bring along great dividends in business. The techniques include:

Saying "Thanks." Show some appreciation for a deed well done. I can count on one hand the number of times I hear the word "Thanks" in a coffeeshop or restaurant in one week.

Looking the person serving you, or the person you are serving, in the eye. What is more distasteful than looking down at your feet while you are talking to someone? The good news for the "foot looker" is that they will probably never have to worry about dealing with the person who endured the lack of eye contact ever again.

Addressing the person by name. Ever wonder why people wear nametags? It's so you can address them by name.

Listening to people. Many of the conversations I have today with young people go in their left ear and out the right one. It's not their fault. They are living in the Age of Rude. Once again, a great opportunity to set yourself apart. Remember, God gave you two ears and one mouth; one of them closes and the other two don't.

Looking like what the customer wants you to look like. Business attire has deteriorated to a nearly comical level. This from the eyes of an old man. However, it is easier to make a good impression without starting by making a bad one with your appearance. Sorry for the verboten, politically incorrect vignette.

Showing appreciation. A sincere "Thank-you" can go a long way—especially today. There are a lot of ways to say thanks. One that I find very effective is a handwritten note. When I receive a thanks on a handwritten note, I really appreciate it and take it to heart. That tells me the receiver of a note I write will feel the same.

Making the EXTRA CALL. If something has gone wrong in your business, do what you have to do, within reason, to make it right. And after you have cajoled, and apologized, and done whatever you had to do to fix the issue, make the extra call. After you have convinced yourself you've done everything you can, make one extra call. Otherwise, all the work you've put into correcting the issue may go for naught.

I have come across a lot of people in my 40-plus-year business career. I hope I have consistently provided courtesy every step of the way, although it is likely I have not. Think of the people you have passed in life, and look over your shoulder at those who became enormous successes. Were you courteous to them?

The dividend that courtesy pays is available to all of us—and it pays a BIG dividend.

Get off the treadmill

Everybody is doing things the same way. Everybody is jumping on the treadmill in lockstep. Companies are latching onto the current popular fads and techniques in customer service in perfect timing with one another. Think about how so many of them are doing things the same way:

- "Listen closely, as our menu options have changed." This engaging, melodious recording can be heard on the phone trees of companies from $1.00 in revenue to $1BILLION.
- "This call may be recorded for quality assurance purposes." Yeah, sure.

- "I can't talk right now; I am with a client." This is the new craze in using texting to avoid answering the phone.
- Portals, secure emails, and all the rest. The wall is up! You can't get in and many, many, many businesses are tickled to death to keep you out.

How is it that so many companies latch onto this stuff so fast? Is there some kind of business czar up there who controls all this? It is uncanny how these methods become the norm almost instantly, throughout all lines of business.

What a fantastic opportunity this drops right at your feet.

Get off the treadmill. Don't buy into these easy-to-use methods. All you are doing is presenting yourself and your company in the exact same manner as your competition. This is yet another opportunity to stand out simply by offering a more hands-on, courtesy-driven welcome to the external customer. So easy to do right now yet so rare in the application.

It is so easy today to stand out from the competition. Look at your business from the customer's point of view—not the same treadmill instruction booklet your competition is reading.

Distinguish your reputation, your company, and your checking account

Over the years, I have dealt with many print, radio, digital, and television marketing concerns. In most cases, the advertising contracts I had with these people supported the mortgage business. I have had great luck with some of the advertising these folks sell.

One of my most successful campaigns was from 2000 to 2006, advertising in the local newspaper, *The Courier-Journal*. I ran an ad every Sunday, Monday, and Wednesday that was placed in the same spot in the paper.

The placement and timing of the ads gave people the impression that they ran daily—a comment I heard from people over and over. All of the ads were about advice and counsel to people buying a home. None of it was the misleading stuff about "no closing costs" or "low fees."

At one point, I did some television advertising and some radio ads as well. The good people who sold these products to me could always tell me how many people the ads would reach. They could as well define the demographics, households, and age groups and even pin down profiles of the people and areas the ads would reach. They could tell you just about everything related to the reach and coverage of the ads. BUT there was one thing they couldn't tell me—which was what, if any, return I would get on my investment. How much money would I get in return for the money I spent on the advertising? That was the question that advertising folks could not answer then or now.

There is another form of advertising that will give you a definable return: word of mouth. The only way word-of-mouth advertising works is if the service provider can present service excellence to the customer. The only way word-of-mouth advertising is effective is if the service provider exceeds the expectations of the external customer. On the other hand, if the service provider does a poor job taking care of the customer, you can bet that the word of mouth resulting from that performance will be extremely damaging.

If I had done a better job over the years of managing my database and customer referrals, I could give you the numbers and statistics about word of mouth. What I do know is this: Very often, in the majority of my cases, the mortgage borrower came to me on the advice of a previous customer. The point is, if you provide customer service excellence, it will make deposits to your checking account, and your reputation, in various ways. One is the time, trouble, and aggravation you will save correcting or curing a service ill. And that means money because time is money.

Another is the money you will save dealing with the aforementioned media advertising. Word of mouth will drive more business to your door than any of the forms of advertising we have discussed. All that those forms of advertising require is writing a check. Word-of-mouth advertising, the most enhancing and sure-to-succeed form of advertising, requires performance. But the results are terrific. If you want to distinguish yourself and your business, customer service is the formula that will get new business in the door. Testimonials from your previous customers about your exemplary customer service is the most effective form of advertising you will ever need—and you don't have to buy it.

Word of mouth: the golden goose in business. The only way to get the golden goose to lay eggs is with superior customer service.

Market share of PKM—it CAN be done!

Sometimes David beats Goliath. And it doesn't just happen in the Bible. Sometimes it happens in business. Sometimes smaller companies beat out the giants for business. I predict this will begin to occur more often than it has in the past due to the current level of terrible customer service. What an opportunity for the business operator who knows how to treat a customer. Here is an example of a small company outperforming a much larger concern.

2002 was the second full year of operation for Paul Karem Mortgage (PKM). We had launched our business with the customer in our sights. I had hired three young ladies, all of whom had touched multiple lines in the mortgage business. They had been processors, senior processors, and underwriters and had done some originating. All three of them today are still enjoying successful careers in the mortgage business. Instead of labeling them as they were titled in their previous positions (underwriter, processor, originator), I decided to try something a little creative. All three carried business cards that said *VP/Underprosinator*. Underprosinator. A combination of the three jobs they previously held, and an acronym (kinda) that described the innovative way they would perform in their new roles.

In the experience of the external customer, these ladies:

- Answered the telephone during all their waking hours, consistent with our No Voice Mail During Office Hours claim
- Processed the loan
- Prepared the loan for underwriting
- Delivered the loan closing docs to the closing

A little different from a lot of our competition, where, at most places, the files went from the originator to setup clerk to processor to loan review to underwriter, back to processor to title agent, and finally, to the closing attorney. With a voice mail recording greeting and frustrating the borrower/client at every stop.

Louisville Business First is a local publication that puts out a Lists of Louisville each year. The list is a ranking of businesses in Louisville, KY, by industry category, from top to bottom. The rankings cover the entire gamut of businesses, including retail stores, insurance companies, banks, healthcare companies, and on and on.

In 2002, my second full year operating Paul Karem Mortgage, my company proudly ranked as the #12 largest mortgage brokerage company in the city. Not a bad position for a company that had been in business for just 2+ years. At the time of the ranking, I had four support staff members—three underprosinators and a terrific receptionist. I was the only salesperson, or mortgage originator, at the time. Five people total.

The 13ᵗʰ ranked company had a support staff of 100 people and 16 mortgage loan originators. With five people, our dollar volume of closed transactions outperformed a company with 111 more people. How did that happen? Was it because we were smarter? Absolutely not! Was it because we had better mortgage products? Absolutely not! As a matter of fact, in spite of some of the ridiculous advertising you hear frequently, mortgage companies all sell pretty much the same apples. That's because the great majority of residential home loans are bought and serviced by the same investors. But that's another story.

The reason we were able to accomplish what we did was that we built the business through the eyes of the customer. No Voice Mail During Office Hours. Underprosinators. We answered the phone—and most of our competition did not, as the heyday of voice mail came into full bloom. We blurred the lines between work, vacation, and home because we got great satisfaction in our work, which stemmed from pleasing people with great service. We woke up the natural spirit of helpfulness, a basic instinct in the human design.

We did all the things you can do simply by administering great internal and external customer service. There has never been a better time than now to gain all the things you dream of simply by becoming a great customer service purveyor.

AND KICK GOLIATH'S BEHIND.

It is all out there for you. Right now.

Want to escape from a dead end job? Customer service excellence is the key

Some years ago, I was the mortgage division manager of a regional bank that was going through the motions of being absorbed by a larger bank.

The forthcoming takeover created havoc at the watercoolers and the coffeepots. People were in near hysteria and panicking over what might happen to their jobs when the bigger bank completed the takeover. I really had never been around a situation quite like this and watched all the nervous gossip and anxious forecasting that went on up and down the halls with a little amazement and a little clarity—because I saw what was really going on. These people were not prepared for a takeover.

The nervous and anxious folks were nervous and anxious because they were unsure of their true value to the eventual owner. Nothing brings on anxiety and doubt like the lack of preparation. Worrying about keeping your job and conveying your trouble to everyone who will listen is probably the absolutely worst way to maintain your position. If you are not prepared for a situation like this, you can bet that tough times are coming down the road. And what is the best way to prepare for takeovers and buyouts and mergers and all the other uncertainty that the market brings forth? Become great at your job. You have to create your own value to avoid situations like this, which are certain to happen sometime in your career.

When you are great at your job, the instance of a takeover is more likely to bring greater opportunity right to your feet. And the best, surest way to be great at your job is to understand how to achieve customer service excellence in your position. The best, surest way to be great at your job is to excel at the things that are critical to customer service. Respond, listen, care, follow up, make the extra call, and look critically at your performance from the customer's eye, not your own eye. Today, it is unlikely that your competition is doing these things or is even aware of the value of them.

Once, when I was at a crossroads in my career, I got some advice from a very smart lady. At the time, I was trying to decide on a job change and was confused. She told me to "design whatever it is that you want." When I asked how to go about doing this, she had me complete a task. The task sounded easy but ended up being quite a struggle for me, as it will be for you if you decide to do this enlightening exercise.

She told me to:

- Write down three things you are great at. Don't be humble—everybody is great at three things, even if it's cooking spaghetti.
- Write down three things you will never tolerate in a job. (This was easy to do at the time because I was very frustrated in the current position.)
- Write down three jobs you would take today (harder than it sounds).

After you've concluded all three steps, read the tea leaves. Make a plan, execute the plan with great effort, and if the plan doesn't work, have the guts to change the plan.

This worked perfectly for me. A surprisingly tough assignment to complete but when finished it gave me the certainty and confidence to start my own company. The answer jumped off the paper and hit me right in the face. It worked very well but it would have failed miserably, as most new businesses do, had I not had a grasp on customer service.

Want to enjoy a business career where the lines are blurred between work, home, and vacation?
Become great at customer service.

Want to surround yourself with inspiring people who will lift you and your career?
Find a place with great customer service.

Want to stand out in your area of profession, regardless of whether it's in technology, sales, management, retail, or whatever in the world it is?

Become great at customer service.

Want to fatten up your wallet?

Become great at customer service.

Want to turn your customers into your sales and marketing force?

Become great at customer service.

Want peace of mind on Sunday night before going to work on Monday?

Become great at customer service.

Want to recruit and surround yourself with the best talent?

Become great at customer service.

Want to glean praise and recognition from those you compete with?

Become great at customer service.

Want the fastest way to recover from a bad financial situation?

Become great at customer service.

America's Customer Service Disaster ... WHAT AN OPPORTUNITY!!!!!

Illustration by Steve Ford down at the Tollhouse